LIBERATING LOUIE

LINDA A MEREDITH

For the wonderful men in my life
Iain, Terry, Chris, Sam and Zachary

PROLOGUE

I dreamt about him again last night…

Just the two of us, happy in each other's company, strolling along, enjoying the scenic beauty of the Rutland countryside. It was the most perfect, summer day; the sun shone down from a cloudless, azure blue sky, and there was no-one around, just him and me.

We were heading down to a little stream; it was one of our favourite places to go during the summer months. A little rickety bridge offered an alternative path across the stream, but we wouldn't be using it today – we would paddle across the ford and cool down.

As soon as he spotted it, he dashed off, only stopping when he landed in the stream with a big splash spraying the water everywhere! I joined him in the cool, refreshing water. It was a welcome relief from the heat.

Once on the other side, we stretched out on a little towel. I put my arm around him and pulled him close. I felt my heart swell with love for him. And there we stayed – nothing to do, nowhere to be, I wanted this day to last forever; I felt totally at peace. He lay his head on my lap and closed his eyes. Hearing a noise in the distance, but not wanting to be disturbed, I snuggled against him and tried to ignore it, but it kept on and on. What on earth was that dammed, irritating noise disturbing our bliss? Much as I didn't want to, I knew I would have to put an end to it.

Reluctantly, I started to open my eyes, and in those few, precious moments before waking, when your dreams and reality feel like one and the same, my world was at peace and happy. That is, until I rolled over, to see Jake's little casket on my bedside table, and realised, I'd been dreaming again....

THE COLD LIGHT OF DAY

My heart deflated as I realised I wasn't in the sunshine cuddling Jake, and that dammed, irritating noise was the alarm clock demanding my attention. I guess I should have been grateful that I'd been to sleep, as I'd found it quite difficult in the past few weeks. I reached out to turn off the alarm, and felt the tears welling up once again. I took his casket to bed with me every night - I just needed to feel he was still near. I'm sure I'm not the first person to have done this, it was comforting to know he was right there beside me during those sad, restless nights, when memories deny you a restful sleep. Knowing he was home again helped me through that awful time.

Unable to jump on the bed anymore, Spike was laid on the floor at my side of the bed, his tail beating in rhythm, waiting for his breakfast. His tail no longer wagged at the speed of light, but there was still plenty of wagginess left in it. I leaned over and stroked his huge head. Thinking aloud I whispered, "Oh my lovely old Spikey boy, I know you're missing him too, how are we going to manage without him?"

Jake

Judging by his response, the only thing Spike seemed to be missing right at that moment was his breakfast. Wearily, I got out of bed, picked up the little casket and went to the stairs. I always walked down in front of Spike these days, as he wasn't as steady on his paws as he used to be. I popped Jake down next to his photo in the living room and went to get Spike's breakfast. Never one to let anything come between him and his food, he got stuck in and scoffed the lot before I'd had time to boil the kettle!

I took my cup of tea and two slices of toast (one for me- one for him) into the conservatory and watched him potter about the garden. Much slower these days due to his arthritis, he mooched around checking to see what, if anything, had been in his garden overnight. When he found the right spot, he squatted down for a pee. He'd given up cocking his leg after falling over a few weeks ago! We didn't laugh (well, only a little bit!)

Old age comes to us all, and it was sad to see that it had caught up with Spike - he was an old man now. At thirteen years of age, his tap staring, water snorting, balloon chasing, stick killing, bath biffing days were behind him, and he was growing old extremely disgracefully and exceptionally stinky! I think he managed to surprise himself with some of the after effects following a good farting session.

Can you imagine if they had Canine Olympics? He wouldn't do too well at running (he only runs if water or taps are involved) he wouldn't do too well at obedience either (my delinquent dog doesn't do obedient)

He'd do pretty well at swimming, but come the Stink-A-thalon, there'd be no competition; a dead cert, he'd win paws down – bronze, silver AND gold! He could produce some absolutely putrid specimens – powerful enough to dissolve the fillings in your teeth! Can you imagine if they did wind surfing!...

Get out of here!!

A prize little stinker maybe, but we loved him. With Spike around, we felt a connection to Jake, just as, in earlier years I had felt a connection to my lovely old dad when Mr. Wigs was here.

I called him in for his toast, but he wasn't quite ready to come in just yet. Watching him wandering around the garden made me realise that one way or another, I was going to have to try and come to terms with losing Jake and go forward; although I knew it wasn't going to be easy, I knew this little soul would help us.

Spike – the comical canine

MOVING ON 2010

Summer was nearing its end, with August having been the coolest on record since 1993! Soon, Mother Nature's kaleidoscope of dazzling colours would proclaim the arrival of Autumn – time to dig those hot-water bottles out for the chilly nights that lay ahead.

We visited The Burghley Horse Trails once again at the beginning of September. Only couple of weeks after losing Jake, it was inevitable the outing would stir up lots of memories, from the happy times we'd spent there in previous years with him and Spike, but I was prepared to risk it. This visit was kind of official, as it was in Iain's capacity of a financial advisor, representing the bank he worked for. It involved entertaining clients in the hospitality tent, however, this invitation did not extend to his wife and dog.

Nevertheless, feeling in need of a little pick-me-up, I'd decided to would go along and amuse myself until the hobnobbing and corporate stuff was finished, then we could mooch around and have some lunch. There's always so many various, delicious cuisines on offer, you're spoiled for choice!

Spike wasn't joining us this time. I knew he would have loved the outing, but he just couldn't walk too well any more.

Iain's parents kindly agreed to have him for the afternoon, so I could go along. We didn't leave him on his own unless it was absolutely necessary, he even came shopping with us (as long as it wasn't too hot) and was happy to lie on the back seat and have a snooze – but only after he'd turned on the hazard flashers! Somehow, he could still manage to pour himself into the front of the car to do this, but was almost always in the back when we returned. He liked going to visit his grandparents so there wouldn't be a problem – or so we thought.

With Spike deposited with the Grandparents, we set off for the short drive to Burghley House in Stamford. Once there, Iain went off in search of the huge marquee the bank had erected, and I went for a quick peek at the stalls. As always, there were so many, offering all kinds of unique and unusual wares. I made a mental list of stalls to visit later with Iain, then, after the allotted time, headed off back to meet him by the huge marquee. He was already waiting for me, and I could tell the minute I saw him he had something on his mind.

I was right…

He wouldn't be able to get away as planned but was hoping not to be too long - clients to smile at, mingling to be done, blah blah blah, so we arranged to meet again thirty minutes later. I knew I would have no trouble at all amusing myself and went back into the crowds.

There are always lots of dogs at the event, but I wasn't quite prepared to come face to face with a Jake lookalike! Like a magnet, I was over in a flash, squatting down to him with the familiar 'Hello Staffy!" greeting! This little guy could have been Jake's twin – even down to the little flash on his chest. He was eleven years old, and his name was Jack!

Can you believe it!?

The poor couple that owned him must have wondered what the hell hit them! I let them have it with both barrels, as they were forced to listen chapter and verse about my Jake (that'll

8

teach them to talk to strange women!) I was very proud of myself for not crying, but as Jack and his owners walked off into the distance, I could feel the tears welling up. Time to go and find Iain.

I must have been bashing their ears for the whole half hour (never) because Iain was waiting for me (again) when I arrived back at the tent. I told him about meeting Jack, and how much he was like our Jakey boy. Trying to cheer me up, he said I couldn't go around accosting everybody with a Red Staffy, then, when he realised, I hadn't actually looked at any of the stalls because I'd been chatting so long, he said the couple were probably over in the first aid tent, being treated for bleeding ears!

What a cheek! He won't be laughing when the 'bed with no beer' card comes out tonight!

He then went on to tell me he'd have to stay longer to entertain his clients, (what a shame!) so perhaps I should go and get myself some lunch, as he would have something from the fancy buffet in the hospitality area. You can imagine how absolutely delighted I was to hear that! Poor lad, having to *force* himself to dine on up-market canapes, and drink free beer - such a martyr! I hope the bank realised how lucky they were to have an employee who went above and beyond the call of duty! He'd have much rather spent his afternoon being dragged from stall to stall by me!

He'd been offered a lift home too – if I wanted to leave? You bet I did! I certainly had no intention of eating lunch alone So, being the dutiful wife (and through gritted teeth) and a smile that would impress any psychopath, I wished him a pleasant afternoon (I so didn't!) and went to collect Spike.

I called Iain's dad and told him I was on my way. When I pulled up on the driveway, I could see the outline of a dog through the glass door. Spike was already waiting for me. They must have told him I was coming! When I went inside, his tail, as always started wagging.

"Hello Spikey, are you waiting for me - did you miss me?" I said as I stroked the top of his head.

Iain's dad told me that unfortunately, Spike had been sat in the same spot since the minute we left. No amount of cajoling or promises of chewies could persuade him to move.

"Have they been beating you little guy" I laughed, knowing full well nothing could be further from the truth

I squatted down, hugged him a little tighter, and told him we were going home for his dinner, which seemed to perk him up. I had intended to stay for a cuppa with them, but the little guy seemed eager to be on his way, so we went out to the car. Considering how bad his arthritis was, he had no trouble whatsoever getting in - He wanted to go home.

"Are you sure you haven't battered him?" I teased as stood by the driver door "seems he can't get away quick enough!" Spike had positioned himself in the front passenger seat and looked straight ahead through one of his glazed expressions. I'm sure if I'd left the keys in the ignition, he'd have set off without me! I thanked them again, waved goodbye and set off for home.

It was only a fifteen- minute journey from their house to ours, and by the time we arrived home, Spike seemed perfectly fine. 'I wonder what that was all about' I said to myself…

The glazed look on his face reminded me of another time that we'd left him with Iain's parents a few years ago. We'd gone to my nephew's wedding and taken Jake with us. Spike however, had to be left behind because he didn't get on with Bobby (Nicky's dog) Jake and Bobby were fine, they'd got on from the minute they'd met. We called them the 'kissing cousins' and they loved to play together.

As for Spike, well he didn't do playing with young whippersnappers, especially when it involved said whippersnapper frolicking with his best bud. Even in his later years, he would have loved to put Bobby dog in his place – right between his jaws I'm guessing! The feeling was mutual, so it was best to leave him at home.

When we went to collect him, we noticed his head seemed to be listing to one side. Iain's dad said that he'd been a bit off the previous night, then they'd come down that morning to find his head slightly favouring one side. Because he wasn't showing any other signs of illness, and knowing we were on our way home, they didn't call the vet.

Back home, he seemed fine, and very happy to see Jake. Spike attended to business straight away, and gave Jake a proper, good biffing! Not sure if it was a 'welcome home' biff, or a 'how dare you leave me' biff. Either or, they were happy to be biffing each other again. Spike made us smile, we watched as he weighed up his line of biff, then missed completely. We didn't laugh though!

First thing Monday morning, I was on the phone making an appointment at the vets. We took him down late afternoon, and after a thorough examination, the vet said there was a possibility of an ear infection but took a blood sample to check all possibilities. One of these was vestibular disease, which appeared to fit all the criteria, and most likely to be the cause of his wobblelyness.

I am not qualified to explain about the vestibular system, but my understanding is it is responsible for controlling eye movement and balance. It can be damaged by disease, aging or injury, and can cause imbalance and disorientation. It can also mimic more serious complaints, such as a stroke or a brain tumour, but hopefully will clear up in a few weeks, although the listing head may be permanent. (as we later found out with Spike) It never truly cleared up for him, but he managed to get around without too much trouble. We were both so thankful to hear it wasn't a stroke, otherwise the outcome could have been very different.

Hearing the word 'damaged' took me back to the time we'd had to leave them in those awful kennels, where not once, but on two, separate occasions his ear was damaged, by what, we are pretty sure, was banging his head against the kennel door – only to be ignored. (it was only after investigations the second time in kennels for exactly the same thing, that we discovered the probable cause!) Even now, it's painful to imagine what my poor little guy must have gone through night after night in that place!

How I wish I could have proved his damaged ears were due to their negligence, but they couldn't have cared less. Claimed not to know anything about him banging his head! Grrrrr makes me sooo cross! As a result of that episode, Spike had ongoing, systematic ear problems. On a better note – those awful kennels have since closed down. Good riddance – it means no other doggies will be ignored!

We managed to get to the end of the year without any major mishaps. I was still desperately missing Jake; I just couldn't get our final moments out of my head. Only a few weeks had passed, but it still felt like yesterday. Anyone who says, "It's just a dog" (**PLEASE DON'T!**) can never have loved or been loved by one of these wonderful animals. If only they knew what they were missing.

Every day, I said a little prayer for Jake and Mr. Wigs, (our beautiful Labrador who went to the Rainbow Bridge in 1995) and thanked God for leaving Spike with us to help ease the pain of losing Jake. Had it not been for him, things could have been a lot worse for both of us.

The original Spike – Amazing Mr. Wigs

ANOTHER YEAR BITES THE DUST

I won't pretend it was easy getting through that first year without Jake, it was anything but seemed to pass in a blur. I wanted so much to talk about him, but each time I did, the conversation ended in tears. It was too painful. Everywhere I looked there were memories which, although happy, also made me sad. When his birthday came around (April 15th) we marked the day by putting a few flowers by his casket and lighting a candle next to his photo.

I thought back to the first time we saw him, he was only a couple of weeks old – and absolutely gorgeous! A tiny, snuggly bundle of red fur and puppy breath! It was love at first sight...

At bedtime, I gave myself a pat on the back for getting through the day without too many tears. The next hurdle would be the first anniversary of him leaving us.

So, come August 17th I was determined not to be sad - he wouldn't want that. I tried to busy myself in the house, but the moment I heard Iain's voice when made his daily morning call, the tears began to flow. I knew he was hurting too. That pain was one of those things only we two could feel, we'd laid either side of our little guy and held him as he left us behind and went to the Rainbow Bridge. No matter how hard I tried not to, my mind insisted on going over and over the events of the day he left. It was truly heart breaking... Why do we do it to ourselves? – insist on replaying memories that bring tears and pain? Someone once told me that pain is the price you pay for love. I really believed it that day.

However, when October arrived, we were in for a nice surprise! Spike was still going strong; all be it slowly. These days, our walks were only now and then and consisted of a short trip around the block. We let him decide when he wanted to go out – he soon let us know if he was up for it!

One day after our trot around the block, I got home to find a message on the phone from the vets asking me to ring them. That was a turn up for the books – them ringing me!! Intrigued, I gave Spike his post walk chewy, then dialled the number.

Sheridan answered the phone, we've known her for years and it was lovely to hear her voice. Not only is she a brilliant vet nurse and lovely young lady, she is also the daughter of a very dear friend of mine, Mary, so that makes her extra special! She is always on hand to give us advice and is amazing with all the animals – and the owners.

After the usual 'how are you' etc., She went on to tell me they were looking for a dog who'd had a blood transfusion to take part in a Christmas campaign on behalf of the Pet Blood Bank U.K. The idea was to create Christmas cards and posters to increase awareness of their organisation, raising some much-needed funds along the way, and they thought of Spike!

"Whoo hoo" I shrieked "how amazing will that be – yes, yes YES!"

Well, I was just a bit excited and delighted to accept. What a great opportunity to give something back to this wonderful, little known organisation who'd played a huge part in saving Spike's life back in February 2010. Until he became ill, I didn't realise that such a thing as the Pet Blood Bank even existed. It's just one of those things - don't know of it till you need it – if you get my drift! She promised to get back to me with all the details and we said goodbye. I couldn't wait to tell Iain that we had a 'pin-up boy' in our midst!

By the time Iain arrived home, I was fit to burst! He greeted me with his usual "hello my love, how was your day?"

"Spike's going to be on Christmas cards and posters" I blurted out "the Pet Blood Bank U.K., and the vets are organising it. They rang our vets and told them they were trying to find a dog in our area who'd had a blood transfusion, and they thought of Spike! Isn't that amazing, he'll be famous. Oh, I can't wait. They're going to ring later with the details of his 'photo-shoot. How brilliant is that?!" My vocal cords were in meltdown as I told Iain (several times and several different ways!) As I paused for breath Iain came out with a cracker.

"And what does *he* think?" he joked nodding towards the settee where Spike was having a nap "Have you spoken to his agent, or does he want their people to call his people?" My husband is a daft as I am!

That evening, we both had a glass of wine (well one of us did – the other one had beer!) with our meal and toasted the success of the campaign for the Blood Bank U.K. The only fly in the ointment we could foresee, was how on *earth* were we going to get Spike to sit still long enough to have a photograph taken??

True to her word, Sheridan called me a few days later with all the details for the shoot, and the venue was only ten minutes away.

Spike's 'pin-up' day dawned bright and sunny, with a slight nip in the air. I packed him up in the car for the short drive to the next village. He loved to ride shotgun, so I strapped him in the front seat and set off. I parked as close as I could get to the village hall and slowly walked him up to the door, where there was a lovely lady waiting to greet us. We chatted away for a while, then she introduced me to Boo – a very handsome German Short Haired pointer, and his mum Nicky. We then met the photographer, who explained what he wanted us to do.

The idea was to position both dogs on this little set they'd created, which had 'snow' on the floor, a Christmas tree at the back, and a large, gift-wrapped box in the middle. The dogs would sit by the tree with the box between them. They would each have a paw on the box, signifying the giving and receiving of a gift. I thought the idea was brilliant and couldn't wait to get started. Persuading Spike onto the set would be easy – getting him to stay there would take a minor miracle, but I had come prepared with a few of his favourite treats in my pocket – just in case!

I turned around expecting to see Spike behind me, but he wasn't there. I did a quick scan of the room and was surprised to find him down the other end chasing a little dog. I couldn't believe my eyes. First of all, he'd got a fair old wiggle on, and although he was experiencing a little four- wheel drift on the polished floor, he was determined to catch him!

I smiled as I watched him skidding about but did a double take when the lady said the dog he was chasing was a cat! I kid you not, that pussy was about the size of a Jack Russell, and a large one at that! It appears he could always be found hanging out at the hall when it was open.

The lady told me that the cat's name was Tank – very apt. Whoever had christened this cat had a good sense of humour! I had never seen such a huge moggy in my entire life, and it seemed Spike couldn't believe his luck either! There was absolutely zero chance of Spike catching it (I'm sure the cat knew this too) so Tank lay down until Spike got close, then moseyed a few feet away, and laid in wait for him again. So cool was this cat, I half expected him to whip out a nail file from his back pocket to sharpen his claws while he chilled and waited for Spike.

The nonchalant cat went on and worked the rest of the hall, stopping alongside his devoted public, so they could all pay homage to him. Then, in full view of his audience, he sat down and proceeded to clean his bits!

I called for Spike, but I was just going through the motions – I knew he couldn't or didn't want to hear me, he was way too interested in the performing pussycat. Eventually, after 'persuading' him with a couple of his favourite treats, I managed to get him to where I wanted him to be. Boo complied immediately, and did exactly as he was told. My turn next, and you guessed it- Spike was going nowhere! I tried to manoeuvre him into position, but he refused to play. Any of you who have tried to move a Staffy that doesn't want to be moved will understand exactly what I'm talking about!

"Oh Spike, you are a one!" I laughed – (manic like) "what *am* I going to do with you?" (I knew exactly what I'd like to do to him that minute – it involved his bum and my foot!)

Eventually, after all requests for him to move had failed, and all the chewies eaten, they decided the only way this was going to work, was if they moved the set. Spike sat looking rather pleased with himself, as they rearranged the little set around him. They could do no more.

Finally, they were ready to take the photograph. I held my breath, closed my eyes and waited. We had been there well over an hour – not what they'd planned at all. I heard the 'click and whiz' of the camera and opened my eyes. To my utter amazement, Spike was where I'd left him – oh joy!! Not only that, they got the shot they wanted within minutes! No-one was more surprised than me, although I joked about the fact that Spike was just waiting for them to get his best side, before he would allow the shot. I know – I should get out more!

Sadly, for whatever reason, the cards never came to fruition however, I do have a wonderful poster to commemorate the occasion; it has pride of place in our little office upstairs, alongside one or two (hundred) other photos of our other beloved boys!

That's not quite the end of this story….

While I was writing, it occurred to me that I ought to give the Pet Blood Bank a courtesy call to tell them of my intentions, and ask if they were happy for me to use the poster – thankfully, they agreed.

I was lucky enough to speak with Maureen, who couldn't have been more helpful. Having told her about the book, she went away, and of her own accord she found the poster, tracked down Boo – the other dog on the poster, and located his mum, Nicky. She also discovered that Boo was Spike's donor! As if that wasn't enough, she arranged to get me some photos of Boo from his mum! Can you believe it! Now thirteen years old, Boo isn't ready for his pipe and slippers just yet! He is still going strong and trains every day!

Maureen, thank you - you are an amazing ambassador for the Pet Blood Bank U.K. Thanks also to Nicky for the beautiful photos!

Handsome Boo – the little guy who saved Spike

Boo with his brothers – all life savers

Boo with Spike -original poster 2010

The logo may have changed for the PBBUK, but that's the only thing. Their amazing work goes on every day, saving the lives of poorly doggys all around the United Kingdom. The not- for-profit charity provides a twenty-four-hour service to Vets in locations around the U.K. They're always looking for volunteers...

As time marched on, Spike plodded along as only he could,

still providing us with a laugh or two. He still tried to attack balloons, but only if they were static so he could kill them at his leisure. Sadly, he didn't have too many teeth left at this point in his life, but it made me howl to watch his new, favoured method of dispensing with the balloons - death by a proper good sucking!

The 'bath' and 'tap' words still grabbed his attention, and even though it was a very slow saunter to the bathroom, his 'glazed stare' look was still fully operational, and he'd beam at the taps until we turned one of them on. No longer able to reach the flow of water, he was content to just sit there mesmerised, watching and whimpering.

He continued to take medication for his arthritis and Viscotears for his eyes. Never once did he get agitated or try to avoid having the drops put in his eyes three times a day, even though it can't have been pleasant for the little guy. He didn't mind having the Rimadyl either, because they came with a little cheese on the side! His EaseFlex chews had never been a problem – he loved them. We gave him Tramadol to ease his pain on the days he seemed to struggle, but there was nothing more we could do. Just like we humans, if the weather was particularly cold, his arthritis played him up.

We had to accept his time was approaching, he was the centre of our world, and we gave him all the love and attention he could possibly need. As we prepared to celebrate Christmas 2011, we both suspected it may be his last: we hoped and prayed that if the coming year was to be his last, we would be spared of having to make that most heart-breaking of decisions, to help him to the Rainbow Bridge...

One in a million...

THE MANCUNIAN MONGREL

When April 15th, 2012 arrived, you would have been forgiven for thinking Spring had been postponed. Winter was clinging on for grim death and it was a miserable, cold, wet day. Upstairs in our little office, I gazed at the rain trickling down the windows, in my own little world, alone with my thoughts. I was waiting for my computer to burst into life, I was going to have a quick game of Shooting Frogs to distract myself from thinking too much about what day it was.

When the computer burst into life, I stared at the screen saver in front of me, and, as I knew they would, tears started to flow - just the odd one to start with, but very soon I was giving the rain a run for its money. For there, staring right back at me was my special little guy – my wonderful, sweet Jakey boy. That aching pain still burned so deep, it felt like I could hardly breathe, because my throat was so constricted as I tried to hold in the tears. But resistance was futile. Especially today.

Jake's birthday had arrived – our second one without him - he would be thirteen years old. I just couldn't divert my eyes from his little face, and soon I was looking for the file that contained the rest of his photos. Even though I was already in tears, I just had to look through them. Isn't it strange how such beautiful photos of happy memories quite often evoke tears? Yet, knowing this, we still have to look at them, we just can't resist.

Sometimes, I swear I'd seen him, just out of the corner of my eye, only to vanish when I turn to see. The overwhelming feeling that he is close to me is almost tangible, and I half expect him to come sauntering through the door looking for a chewy. I wonder if he knows that sometimes I feel my heart will break through the heartache of losing him. Does he know that today is especially hard? I believe he would help me if he could; he wouldn't want me to be sad.

Lucky for me, Spike, who was sprawled across the landing snoring his head off, chose that very moment to throw a little comedy into the proceedings, as he relived himself of an award-winning fart, and woke himself up! I went across to hug him, but mindful what he'd just done, I went easy on the hugs and tried not to squeeze (or breathe) too deeply! I often wondered what he thought about Jake not being around anymore – did he know what had happened?

Just then the phone rang, so I quickly blew my nose and answered it. It was Nicky, she never forgets Jake's birthday bless her, but today, there was something else on her mind today too, and she thought I might be able to help. She went on to tell me a very distressing tale…

She'd been to the vets with Bobby and got herself involved in another rescue mission – (went in with one dog and came out with two!) As you would imagine, she spends so much time ferrying cats, dogs and anything else she can get her hands on to the vets', she is on first name terms with most of the staff. Whilst waiting to book Bobby in, she was having a chat with Elaine, the Senior Practice Administrator. Elaine broke off their chat to take a phone call, which, when it ended, left her visibly distressed.

Nicky asked what was wrong, and Elaine disclosed the details of the phone call. There was a chap bringing a dog in to be euthanised – it was perfectly healthy and only two years old. What was making Elaine even more upset, was the fact that this wasn't the first time this had happened. The chap had brought the same dog in a few months ago for the same thing, only to change his mind at the last minute, and take the dog home again!

The last thing any vet wants to do, is euthanise a healthy pet – and only when there is no hope, and the list of options has been well and truly exhausted for sick animals do they consider this. The thought of sending a perfectly healthy, two-year-old dog to Rainbow Bridge is inconceivable! Elaine needed a plan – and fast, as the dog was already on its way!

Luckily for her, the plan stood right in front of her, in a dark, soggy raincoat with a Border Collie! Step forward Stalybridge's answer to International Rescue - NICKY!!

"I just can't stand by and let this happen, I have to do something. It's not right, he's little more than a pup, so sweet and loving. You should have seen him when he was here before, laying on his back so we could rub his tummy, we all fell in love with him. Why would anybody in their right mind want to do a thing like this, I just don't understand!" cried Elaine

Nicky was devastated with what Elaine had told her, so between the two of them, after a lot of discussion, they came up with a possible solution, however, that solution was a hundred and twenty miles away in Rutland!

"So, I was wondering if there was any possibility that you could have him? I know it's a bit short notice, but we really are desperate, and time is against us. Elaine has told the owner there may not be a vet available till two-o-clock, but he's still coming, so she's going to see if she can work something out, but we need to act fast"

No pressure then, after all, the only thing that stood between us and the dog was a hundred and twenty miles, and two and a half hours - no problem at all Nick!

"Poor little soul" I responded ", how could anyone even

think about ending the little guy's life for no reason. I'll have to speak to Iain, obviously, but it's Spike who's my main concern, I don't want him getting upset because we're moving a younger model in. By the way, what kind of dog is it? Not that it makes any difference under the circumstances..."

"He's a black Staffy with a bit of bindle, and his name is 'Taco' I remembered you said that if you ever had another one, it would have to be black, so you wouldn't be tempted to compare it with either of the lads. You can always change his name. He could be your Louie!"

Oh, you just bet he could – black Staffy – ahhhh... music to my ears!

We decided long ago that the little Black Staffy, who was waiting somewhere in the future for us would be called Louie.

"Give me a few minutes to speak to Iain, and I'll call you back. Don't give up on me, it might be difficult to speak to him if he's in a meeting, or en route somewhere. Don't move!" I told her "I'll be as quick as I can"

With that, I hung up the phone, and went to my bedroom in search of my mobile to call Iain. I bumped into Terry at the top of the stairs. He and Marcia, (his fiancée at the time) were staying with us for a while en route to Texas. They had spent a couple of years in Egypt and were now moving on to pastures new in Houston, which is where Marcia comes from.

"Eh up Bid, what's going on?" (my sons always refer to me as The Bid, or Biddy) he asked as he followed me into my bedroom. I picked up my mobile and pressed the speed-dial for Iain

While I waited to be connected, I gave him edited highlights of Nicky's call.

"What about Meathead?" he asked, using one of Spike's many aliases

Just then, I heard Iain's voice message come on – Damn!! I left a message to call me asap. Not content with that, I tried his number again – just in case.

"Well, I haven't really had much time to think about that, but

25

I guess if they don't get along, and we can't find a good home for him, we can take him to the Dogs' Trust or the Animal Rescue place near Peterborough. What do you think?"

"Well, it's infinitely better than the alternative" he remarked

"When are you going to get him? Assuming Iain says it's ok"

"Oh ye of little faith – do you really think he's going to say no? I have an arsenal of resources to help him make up his mind, though I doubt he'll say no under the circumstances" I told him.

Just then, our conversation was interrupted by my mobile – it was Iain. I grabbed the phone from my pocket and swiped to answer.

"Hello, my darling, what's the matter?" he asked in his 'what have you broken' voice

"Well, you won't believe this, but…"

I related the story of the dog as quickly as my mouth would let me (it can fairly move when it wants to - nought to sixty in ten seconds!)

"So, you see, this little fella is really desperate, what do you think?" I finished.

It was quiet at the other end of the phone. I could imagine Iain weighing up the pros and cons of another dog. Finally, he spoke

"What about Spike? What happens if they don't get on? He needs all our attention at the moment"

Spike's welfare was paramount to all of us; at almost fifteen we knew his days were numbered. I dared not think about losing him too…

"Already thought about that (well, almost) there's a Dog's Trust in Leicester, if he doesn't get on with Spike, and if we can't rehome him ourselves, we'll take him there. Spike will still get all the attention he wants, and it'll stop this poor dog being put to sleep… (then in the practised, quiet, pitiful voice) he's only a baby… he's only two… he's called Louie… (okay, so he wasn't really, but it was only a *little* fib – he would be by the time he got home!) Terry's offered to help out too, haven't you Terry?"

"Have I?" Terry silently mouthed "When did I do that?"

"Shhhhhush" I whispered. He disappeared back to his room.

I waited with bated breath for Iain's reply...

"Well, you'd better get a wiggle on and get up the road. Let me know when you arrive at Nickys" I punched the air in delight – result!

"That's the first thing I'll do when I get there. Thanks bud, you're saving this little dogs' life. Now clear off, I'm out of here!" I rang Nicky's mobile to tell her the good news.

"Oh, that's wonderful" she gushed "I'm so pleased Iain said yes"

"Do you really think that would have made a difference?" I giggled "I'll be on my way in ten minutes – bye for now"

To no one in particular, I thought aloud "shoes, best take a cardigan, this one, that one? I'll just put some clean jeans and a top on, long sleeves, short ones, will I need my raincoat?

As I rummaged around the bottom of my wardrobe for a pair of flat shoes, Terry reappeared with a proposal.

"Mum, I was just thinking - you don't need to go and pick the dog up, me and Marcia will go and fetch him if you want?" I stopped for a moment to think about it. To be honest, that would be a much better idea. What if he was travel sick or something? It would be difficult to drive and look after a sick doggy at the same time. Terry was insured to drive my car, so there was no problem. He is possibly a far better (and infinitely more patient) driver than I am – but don't tell him I said so!

"Now that's a brilliant idea, we might need two pairs of hands to look after him in the car. He might need a cuddle, after all, this poor little man's going to be so confused as to what's happening and being taken away from everything he knows by strange people" At this remark, Terry intervened.

"If he thinks me and Marcia are strange, God help him when he meets the rest of the clan!"

"You are a very naughty, bad, disrespectful boy" I teased "Yeah, you go and get him, and I'll stay with Spike and try and get organised for the little guy. I'll get dinner sorted too and we can eat when we've sorted Louie out"

"Yeah, I heard that, is he really called Louie?"

"He is now - I'm not too keen on the name he has. If he doesn't respond to Louie, we'll have to think of something else.

"So, what *is* his name then?"

"Taco" I replied

He gave me a quizzical look, wrinkled his forehead, then said "Louie it is then Bid!" I laughed at his response, "we'll get going then, we need to get him away from there as quickly as possible, just in case this bloke changes his mind – again!"

And that was that – roughly within thirty minutes of Nicky's phone call, I was waving them off. All being well, they could be back later that evening with our new fur-baby. All I could do now, was pray that the new kid would get on with Spike, I didn't want to think about what we'd have to do if he didn't. One thing I was 100% sure of, was that even if he didn't get on with Spike, he would *not* be going to Rainbow Bridge – not till it was his time to go anyway. We'd figure something out for this poor little soul...

After waving them off, I went indoors and rang Nicky to tell her, it wouldn't be me picking him up after all. She was panicking because the guy and 'Louie' had just arrived at the vets. Elaine, ever the professional, was calmly trying her best to dissuade the man from doing something that could never be undone, but he was adamant that this was what he wanted - wouldn't even consider rehoming him. He refused to give a reason, and said that if she wouldn't oblige, he would go elsewhere... That sent me into panic mode! I hadn't even met this little guy, but I loved him already. How could anyone even contemplate such a heinous thing? The more I see the reprehensible side of the human race, the more I love animals!

I wanted to give Louie the loving, happy life that would appear he'd been denied. It might buck Spike up a bit too, having another dog around. Years ago, he wouldn't have tolerated another dog walking past the house on the opposite side of the road, let alone inside his house, but bless his heart, those days were behind him now. Maybe he couldn't sort out these young pups any more, but he'd probably still have a go at giving them a good biffing - and a damn good suck!

Nicky had said she would ring when she had more news and told me not to worry. I prayed Louie would be waiting for them when they arrived. In the meantime, I tried to occupy my mind.

I went in search of some old dog blankets and popped them in the washer, so at least he'd have a clean bed. I found the ones that had belonged to Jake; unwashed but folded up neatly in a bag in the garage – just as he'd left them. I hadn't had the heart to wash them after he'd gone, I didn't want to wash him away! Part of me felt sad and guilty for washing them now, but I'm sure he'd be delighted to see them being put to good use again. I kept just one though – I couldn't wash him all away...

The hands on the clock were moving far too slowly, and much as I willed the phone to ring, it remained silent. No amount of staring at it would make it ring! It was one thirty now, so Terry and Marcia should be almost there. I made myself a cup of tea and went to sit with Spike. As I stroked him, I told him all about this little doggie who seemed to have nobody to love or care for him, so, as long as it was okay with him, the little dog could stay with us. He looked at me as if he understood every word I was saying, but I'm sure if he could have replied, he would have said

"We getting a dog then?"

Finally, around ten minutes later the phone rang, and I leapt from the settee to answer it.

"Hiya, it's me" came the welcome sound of Nicky's voice "Sorry to have taken so long, but we've had a right performance"

I interrupted her "Have you got him? Is he with you?"

"Yes, he's here bless him, safe and sound, but I think he's upset. I've had to leave him in the back of the car (not knowing how he'd get on with the other dogs in the house she was looking after, she thought it was for the best) I've taken a photo of him, I'll send in a minute. Poor little guy looks petrified!"

I raised my face to the sky, and offered a silent 'Thank You'

"That's wonderful news! Thank you so much Nicky"

"Thank YOU!" she replied "You've saved his life. The chap who brought him in was adamant about him being put to sleep, but Elaine worked her magic, and he's safe" Elaine deserved a medal!

She recounted the events that had taken place with Louie's previous, callous owner at the vets. After a lot of conferring between Elaine, a vet nurse and the dog's owner, it was mutually decided that 'Taco' would be 'signed over' in a disclaimer form to the vets, ready for when the vet had a break in his schedule. They were extremely busy with appointments that day, so it might be some time. So, if the owner wanted to leave, they would keep him in a kennel at the back. Thankfully, the chap agreed. He signed the form that Elaine had expertly compiled, and without so much as a backward glance, he stormed out slamming the door behind him...

It was then, that Nicky and Elaine's 'Operation Louie' plan sprang into action. While Nicky followed the chap back to his car, Elaine took Louie into the back, and found a collar and lead for him. Being a fellow pet lover herself, she had gained herself a worthy reputation within the community for rehoming unwanted animals, which she had done many times before.

In this crazy world of disposable pets (buy a dog/cat/rabbit for Christmas and change your mind for New year!) it was wonderful to know there were still genuinely kind and caring people who put the animal's welfare first and foremost. Wonderful people like Elaine, who to my mind, deserve recognition!

Nicky had watched until the chap's car had disappeared, then returned with a big smile on her face.

"He's gone" she shouted

By now, Elaine and Louie were waiting for her, and it was time to get moving – just in case! Elaine bent to give Louie a huge hug, wished him a long and happy life, then accompanied the two of them to Nicky's car. With Louie safely strapped in the back, Nicky revved up the engine ready to go. Elaine was scanning around to make sure his previous owner hadn't changed his mind and was coming back for him! Happily, someone was looking out for Louie that day, and they left the vets without any incidents.

Terry and Marcia arrived at Nicky's not long after she'd got home. She told them all about Louie's previous owner, and the covert operation to get Louie away from the vets over a cup of coffee and a cream cake. I can guarantee, no matter what, if Nicky's expecting company, there will be cake, along with biscuits, and a plethora of tempting treats produced on their arrival. Attempts to leave before eating any of these treats is futile – she won't take no for an answer! Meanwhile, my mobile alerted me to the photo that Nicky had sent – I couldn't open it quick enough.

The slightly, grainy image revealed a dog alright, but it wasn't *quite* what I expected to see! He was certainly different from any other Staffy I'd ever seen. Perhaps because the photo had been taken through the back window of the car might make a difference? I'd just have to wait till he was here and check him out.

At last, Nicky rang to tell me that the mission was complete, the rescue party had departed complete with the precious cargo and were en route to Rutland. Their E.T.A. was between six thirty and seven, depending on the traffic. I couldn't wait!

A few minutes after Nicky's call, Marcia rang to tell me they were on their way. Louie was strapped in the back but seemed very nervous. Just as she was about to tell me more, we lost the signal – they must be on the Pennines, the signal was almost non-existent up there. Drat!

I would just have to be patient until they got here. I told myself not to worry about him being nervous, the main thing was, he was alive and on his way home!!

Maybe Jake *had* had a paw in today's events after all...

Mr. Louie

THE STAFF HAS LANDED

Iain arrived home from work about five thirty, ready for his cup of tea – as usual. While we were waiting for the tea to brew, he went over to where Spike was sitting, waiting for his daily fuss. He still made the effort to greet Iain when he came home, albeit much slower and quieter. While he rubbed Spike's ears, I chatted away about the drama earlier in the day. Then I remembered the photo Nicky had sent and opened it to show him.

"Here he is – what do you think?"

He studied the photo for a few seconds before saying

"I can't really tell from this, but he doesn't look like I thought he would. We'll be able to tell better when he's here. What time are you expecting them?"

"They could be here in about an hour if the roads were clear. Let's give Spike his dinner before they get here, so he can eat in peace"

Spike's hearing might not be as sharp as it used to be, but he still heard the word 'dinner' and started to make his way to the kitchen. Leaving him to eat, we went upstairs so Iain could change, and I could look out of the window for Louie. I gave up after a while and went downstairs to watch the latest news with

Iain. Despite the dramatic events of the day, there was nothing on the bulletin about a 'Dog-napping' incident in Stalybridge!

After what seemed like forever, I heard the car pulling up outside the front of our house. Iain and I flew out, playfully jostling each other to be first down the path - both eager to get a look at our new baby. He seemed a little hesitant to get out of the car at first. I had to remind myself that this little lad had gone through a lot, and maybe didn't feel like meeting any more strangers today! Although I was desperate to get my hands on him, I resisted the urge to snuggle him to death and said 'hello Louie' then stood back to give him some space, as he walked through the gate with Marcia.

As soon as he was in the garden, he cocked his leg, several times, then took a huge dump right in the middle of the lawn before going back to stand behind Marcia. She had been the one comforting him on the journey, and he obviously felt safe with her. She'd gone and sat in the back with him on the way home. That was a good start.

"Good grief" I joked when I saw the mammoth deposit he'd dumped on the lawn "he must have been saving that all week for us. I'll have to get a black bin liner for that lot!'

I studied him as he tried to hide behind Marcia, his tail firmly between his legs, he seemed so upset, but that was to be expected after the day he'd had. He sort of looked like the photo Nicky had sent but didn't look like a Staffy. He was mainly black, with brindle legs and huge, white feet. The brindle also framed his face, and a pair of little white eyebrows completed the look. Tall, slim and sleek, his coat was very shiny and soft, but the only bit of him that could be classed as Staffy, was the little white flash on his chest. His parentage was definitely questionable!

A passing resemblance was nearer the mark. I think the nearest his mum/dad had been to a Staffy was a fleeting glance across a crowded street one day! He looked more like he was crossed with a Whippet and A.N. Other than a Staffy, however, as we would find out, there was no doubt whatsoever that he was as daft as a Staffy!

By this time, Spike had made his way to the front door and stood, wagging his tail waiting to see what all the fuss was about. Louie cowered away and seemed to freeze as Spike was giving him the once over. Luckily, he didn't seem to mind this new kid coming to his house, but Louie seemed very hesitant. With no prospect of Spike moving anytime soon, we bribed him away from the door with a promise he could look at the tap, and offered him a chew, which he readily accepted. So, with Spike and his chewy staring at his beloved taps, we encouraged Louie to come into the house.

We filtered into the living room and sat down. Louie stayed quivering beside Marcia's leg, and showed little interest in anything else. The poor lad seemed so wary, it must have been a real, upsetting day for him and now he was here, where everything and everyone was strange and alien. With no familiar smells he just didn't understand what was going on. I so wanted to pick him up, snuggle him and tell him everything was going to be fine, but that could have made things worse. I'd just have to be patient, which I find incredibly hard - I don't do patient.

I'd put Jake's old blanket in a corner of the living room for him, but he just wasn't interested. He wouldn't even look at us. When Spike came out of the bathroom, he tried to hide between Marcia's legs, the poor little guy was terrified! Thankfully, Spike didn't seem to mind him being there, and gave him a casual biff as he passed!

Eventually, Marcia persuaded him from behind her legs, and onto his blanket by moving it beside her. This seemed acceptable, as long as she stayed beside him. If she moved – he moved; she went outside for a cigarette; he was right behind her. She went to make coffee; and there he was again! Marcia's little shadow! Cute as it was to be followed everywhere, Marcia drew the line when he followed her to the bathroom – AND- opened the door on her! The last thing she'd expected to see as she went about her business was the dog making a grand entrance through the bathroom door!

We thought perhaps she hadn't shut the door properly, but she said she had, so she went back again to see what happened. Within seconds of her leaving the room, he was after her. She went inside the bathroom and closed the door. We watched in amazement, as he stood up on his back legs, and pushed the door handle down with his paw!

"Well I've seen it all now" laughed Terry "he'll be wanting his own door key next! I wonder what other tricks he can do?"

Did I want to know???

Spike was eager to give Louie the once over, but again, Louie seemed quite timid when Spike got close, and adopted the submissive position. He let Spike give him give him a good sniff and a little biff, before retreating behind Marcia's legs -again! Afterwards, he gave Spike a wide berth when he needed to pass by, but Spike didn't seem to notice as he snored away.

After trying and failing to get him into the kitchen to eat, Marcia finally persuaded him to go with her, and I could hear him having a good slurp from the water bowl. I'd put some food down for him earlier and was pleased to see an empty bowl when I went in later. I told Marcia I was happy to see that he'd eaten the bit of food I'd put down for him.

"Oh, Louie didn't eat anything" Marcia said "there was only the water there"

"Really?" I quizzed "Mmmm I wonder what happened to the food then – Spike!!"

The little gutsy puss had sloped off and scoffed the lot while we were preoccupied with Louie. Spike makes and enforces his own rules-:

If it's there – it's mine...
If I see it... it's mine...
If you see it... it's mine
If you want it...it's mine...
If it's yours...it's mine!
If it's broken – it's mine- after you've fixed it!

That first night, we all headed off for bed, leaving Louie downstairs with Spike. However, no sooner had we settled down than there was the most awful, mournful, distressing sound from downstairs; it was Louie. Never before had I heard such pitiful howling come from a dog. Poor little guy, I was down the stairs in a heartbeat! He still wasn't too keen on coming to me, but seeing as how there was no-one else around, he reluctantly came to me. I stroked him, and talked softly to him, but he just wasn't interested. Spike was snoring away in his pit, unaware of what was going on. I carried on stroking him, until he was quiet, but the minute I got to the bottom of the stairs, the howling started again. Unable to console him, I took him up to bed with me – just for the first few nights (I thought) until he gets used to us and finds his paws. Big mistake!

Talk about rod for my own back, definitely not one of my better ideas! He was on the bed before I'd had chance to pull back the quilt and didn't want to move! I just wanted to sleep and was in no mood for a tete a tete with a dog, so I just climbed in and tried to nod off. Very soon I was regretting the decision to let him on the bed. I could feel him moving around and popped the lamp on to see what he was up to.

He's one of those dogs who has to circle a few dozen times before settling down! He was here, there and everywhere during that night. He was trying to scoop the quilt up and make some kind of nest! "I think not young man" I said through gritted teeth "My bed – not yours – MINE!"

He cocked his head to one side as though he was listening to every word I said. Perhaps he was, but he hadn't a clue what I was saying! By the time morning arrived, he was sleeping peacefully in between the two of us. As Iain got up, Louie wasted no time moving into the warm spot Iain had left. He turned around a few times, then settled down for some more sleep. As I looked at him, I voiced my thoughts, and said 'make the most of this Lou Lou, you'll be in your own bed tonight!'

Contrary to my idea, Louie had his own; and it didn't involve his bed!

Guess who's sleeping in your bed?

38

He spent the next couple of weeks finding his paws. He became more relaxed and we got to know each other. He still gave Spike a wide berth every time he passed him, and Spike continued to side swipe him with a biff whenever the opportunity arose. Louie appeared happy to be second in command and was coming on leaps and bounds. His tail found it's wag, and he started to play with a couple of the toys we'd bought him, however, bedtime continued to pose a problem. If we left him downstairs – he'd howl the house down, and if we took him up – we didn't get much sleep because of Disco Dog boogieing the night away! I had created a dilemma that was going to take time to solve.

Night after night, we ended up with Louie on our bed, strutting his stuff while we desperately tried to sleep. Iain could sleep on a clothes line, but I found it difficult to sleep. By now it was mid-May, and the temperature was starting to rise – just what we needed through the night! As for Spike... well, he didn't care how warm is was, he could (and did) sleep anywhere, and he was doing an awful lot of it lately...

Old timer

A SAD HAPPY BIRTHDAY

It was almost the end of May and it was Marcia's birthday. The day had started gloriously; the sun shone down from a clear blue sky - it was going to be a beautiful day. Even at this early hour, the sun was cracking the flags. Spike was out in the garden, sunning himself in his favourite spot below the conservatory window, and Louie was – well, being Louie and making the garden his own. A tinkle here and a pile there, he seemed to be putting his smell on every single blade of grass! I doubt he'd had a garden in his last home judging by the way he was in ours. He'd learned that Spike was no threat to him, so was now getting a bit cheeky!

Nicky seemed to think he'd lived in a tower block with a window box, which had made me wonder if that's why they wanted to get rid of him? I thought about the consequences of living in a high rise and imagined him cocking his leg and peeing into a little window box on a balcony!

He chased anything that moved, and after almost five weeks with us, he was feeling confident enough to take over 'barking duties' from Spike, whenever anyone passed the house! Spike had obviously decided a few weeks ago to relinquish some of his duties as top dog. He was applying the old 'why have a dog and bark yourself' adage! I think he'd secretly been passing on all his experience with a wealth of expertise and tips to Louie. Hallowed doggy rituals and traditions that are passed on to each new generation. I envisaged they'd go along the lines of...

1. To Pee or not to pee – the question and the answer.
2. Turn the fart to an art.
3. Scrounging for beginners – easy when you know how!
4. The ethic of pathetic.
5. In pursue of the chew.
6. The joy of stinking – be an award winner!

You'll need to perfect all these if you want to be top-dog. Crack on lad!

That morning, Iain, Marcia and me were home, but Terry was working. He'd got a job driving H.G.Vs again to earn some money for their trip to Texas. Once there, he would be unable to work for a while, so was trying to build up a fund. He'd passed his H.V.G test many years ago, and once worked for the prestigious firm with the green livery and named lorries! However, when they relocated to a depot in the west midlands, it was simply too far for him to commute every day. Getting home always depended on the amount of traffic about, but hopefully tonight, there would be no traffic jams or breakdowns, and he would be home in plenty of time to celebrate Marcia's birthday.

As the temperature was rising steadily, we decided to take Louie for his walk before it became too hot. I went to check on Spike – he wasn't going anywhere; he was snoring like a piggy in his favourite spot in a nice bit of shade. There was a nice little breeze by the corner of the conservatory, and he was spread-eagled there on his blanket. I got the parasol from the shed, and angled it over him, just for a little extra bit of protection. The sun wasn't on him yet but may have moved around by the time we got back. He didn't even look up when we left, he was fast asleep.

We drove to one of our favoured walks in a nearby village. It only took us a few minutes, and once out of the car, it was perfectly safe to let Louie have a good run – which he did! He sped off like a heat seeking missile! I shouted him to come back, I didn't want him running that fast in the stifling heat. He came back, but only when he'd finished sniffing something horrible in the hedge!

Just then, I heard my phone ringing. It was Marcia.

Hello chickadee are you alright?"

"Bid, do you think you could come home? I'm a bit concerned about Spike – he seems to be breathing strangely. He seems ok, but it's just this breathing…"

"We're on our way" I shouted "We'll be with you in a few minutes"

We hurried back to the car, strapped Louie in the back and drove home. "Maybe he's just a bit overheated" I thought out loud

"Well, it is quite warm today. We'll get his pool out for him when we get home, he'll soon be cool" Iain stated

Within ten minutes, we were walking through our front door to be met by a very worried looking Marcia, who said,

"He's still in the garden, I didn't want to move him"

We ran through the house, and out the other side into the back garden where he lay.

"Hey little guy, what's the matter with my boy" I cried as I knelt down beside him "what's to do buddy?"

He looked at me, and his little tail began to wag. Just as Marcia had said, his breathing seemed laboured. We both got down and started stroking him.

"Let's get him in the kitchen Iain, the floor's nice and cold, it'll cool him down"

Once in Iain's arms, he began to tremble. As he hurried to the kitchen, Marcia and me were right behind. Somewhere between the garden and the kitchen, he went still. By the time he lay him on the floor, he was gone – just like that - in the blink of an eye he slipped away...

I screamed, "Spike, Spikey boy, come on lad, we're here sweetie, it's okay now, we'll take care of you. Spike, **SPIKE**, come on bud, come on sweetheart, please, *PLEASE* wake up for me little guy. Spike, let's go and see the bathroom taps!!" I was neigh on hysterical by now, Marcia and Iain weren't faring too well either. His small body, convulsed a little, giving the impression that he was okay, but he wasn't. I ran to the phone and rang the vets.

I went into manic mode – Iain told me later what I'd said

"Please help me, my dog's dying, please, what do I do – don't let him die. I don't know what to do" Help, PLEASE HELP ME!" I was totally inarticulate, and garbled all my words

I have no idea why I rang the vets, what could they do? The only bit I remember, is the vet saying 'bring him down'...

I looked down at him, his little body so still now. There was no doubt that he had gone. We knelt beside him and hugged him, then we hugged each other. Crying doesn't come close – I was beyond devastated, we all were, we were absolutely heartbroken...

This was the end of an era – a beautiful chapter of our lives had closed.

The was the end of my beloved boys. As long as we had Spike, we felt a connection with Jake too, but no more. From now on, all we'd have were memories- beautiful precious memories, of the special little guys we'd lost...

The Management

All this time, Louie had been watching the goings on from under the breakfast bar. Somebody once told me if you have more than one cat/dog and one of them dies, let the other one(s) look at the one who's passed away, and it may help them to understand what's happened. With this in mind, we let Louie go to Spike. He sniffed every inch of him, even gave him a little nudge, before walking out to the garden. I would love to think it had helped him to take in what had happened...

We washed our faces, blew our noses and took Spike for his last ever ride in the car. Those of you who have read Fully Staffed, will know how much he loved to go in the car. I held him like a baby on my lap and snuggled him as tightly as I could. I sobbed uncontrollably into his thick, furry neck, something he would only have let me do under sufferance and on his own terms whilst alive. How ironic his last trip in the car would be like this.

The vet was waiting for us when we arrived, clearly distressed to see Spike had gone - saddened for the loss of this remarkable, unique, comical little guy, who had delighted all of them at one time or another with his hilarious antics, who now lay so still in Iain's arms. Catriona, our lovely young Vet took her stethoscope and listened for his heartbeat, but the precious little heart that had given so much love, laughter, joy and happiness, was no longer beating. He'd gone to be reunited with Jake…

We didn't know what had finally ended his life, there was no point in speculating. We told ourselves he'd died of old age – it was easier that way. It is of small consolation to know he hadn't suffered, and, most importantly, we were with him at the end.

We now faced the hardest part of all – leaving him. That last hug brings overwhelming sorrow, but you can't leave without it. With tears flowing out of control, I leaned over and squeezed him as hard as I could for our final hug on earth. I thanked him for all the fun and laughter he brought to our lives. The broken taps, dead balloons, all the scratches in the bath and the total chaos he brought with him.

For one last time, I bent and whispered in his ear – 'Go find Jake little man, he'll be waiting to take you to the bridge. You'll meet your namesake too – the original Spike – Mr. Wigs. There's the biggest tap you ever did see, in a bath that goes on forever, and millions of balloons and gallons of water, just waiting for you. Give them all our love and tell them how much we miss them. See you when we get there little guy, one day we'll all be together again. Till the next time…

Best buddies – together again

We were both silent on the way home, we'd done this drive twice before and today was no less painful. Memories of losing Mr. Wigs and Jake overwhelmed me adding to the anguish of the day. Poor Marcia, we would forever associate her special day with losing Spike.

When we arrived home, Louie greeted our arrival with a waggy tail and lots of barking, Marcia was on hand with hugs and tea. No words were necessary, we all felt the same way. Sooner or later, Terry would be home – he would be shattered to hear the news, after all, there had been no indication that Spike would be gone when Terry left for work.

What concerned me more was Chris. There had been no warning signs that Spike was going to leave us, and I was dreading telling him – he would be absolutely distraught... I hate being the bearer of bad news.

I was going to have to tell the family too, but I had to tell the boys first.

I thought back to the day Jake died. Within an hour of getting back from the vets, there was a friend at the door with some flowers – a wonderful, kind gesture, but I was perplexed as to how she'd found out so soon? The little boy had only been gone a couple of hours! Turns out social media had broken the news. Chris had posted on that well known, societal site after we'd told him; within hours we were inundated with messages of sympathy. I wasn't really too thrilled about this, even though his intentions were good, and the messages were welcome, but I needed to tell Terry and the rest of the family before the news went live on-line, I couldn't let him find out that way!!

Terry was working in Egypt at the time Jake died and was sometimes difficult to get hold of. Jake was very special to him, and although he knew he was very sick, it would still be a shock to hear he'd gone. We communicated via the website, which I knew he checked every day. Thankfully, we managed to tell him and the rest of the family before they saw it 'on-line' I find social media can sometimes be a curse as well as a blessing.

So now we had to do it all again. Spike was quite a popular little guy, had his own fan club, even his own Facebook page! (yes, guilty as charged!) I called Chris's number, and waited for him to answer. On and on the ringing went till finally, his answer phone kicked into action. "if you would like to leave a message…" Er, no – I don't think so. I knew he was at work, but sometimes I can catch him on a break, but not today.

Terry arrived home around sixish, and Marcia broke the news. He was absolutely gutted. We all shed a few more tears, then sat with a cup of tea reminiscing. So many lovely memories… However, we still had to tell Chris – I tried his number again.

This time, he answered his phone after a couple of rings

"Hello, bid, how's it going?" his cheery greeting enquired

"Hello love, where are you?" I needed to be sure he wasn't in the car on his way home

"I've just got home, why – what's the matter?"

He could tell straight away something was wrong, but I knew he had no inkling of what

"It's Spike sweetheart, I'm so sorry to have to be the one to tell you, but he's gone… he passed away at lunchtime…I'm so, so sorry…"

Nothing but silence on the other end, understandable really-then,

"What happened?"

I related the events of the day, the words sticking in my throat, I knew what I was saying would be breaking my son's heart, and it was breaking mine too. Eventually, Iain took over the call, I couldn't talk for the tears that were threatening to choke me.

When Iain got off the phone, he told me Chris was on his way over. He lived close by, so it wouldn't take him long to get here.

Meanwhile, it was time to ring the rest of the family...

Every call was met with tears and sympathy, he was loved by everyone. Chris arrived in between calls, and we stood and hugged each other, sobbing in mutual grief. Weeping for this unique, irreplaceable little guy who meant the world to all of us and would be missed so very much – there would never be another one like him, he truly was beyond compare. He had brought a sense of purpose and restraint to Chris, at a time when he was alone. Together, they had travelled the length and breadth of the country, getting into the occasional scrape on the way. He was in bits...

After all the phone calls had been made, we decided we would open a bottle of wine, after all, it was Marcia's birthday! We could raise a glass to Marcia and Spike, and relive some of the funnier things he had done. There were so many to choose from, it was hard to know where to begin...

One dog and his man

SPIKE'S AWAY-DAY

None of us felt much like eating, so I put out a load of nibbles to keep us going. Terry & Marcia hadn't planned to go out, so we sat around with a glass (or 3!) of wine and reminisced about some of the comical things he'd got up to in his fifteen years on earth.

I remembered a tale that Chris had told us years ago that had us in stiches! It would make us all smile to hear it again, so I decided to remind them all of it...

As previously mentioned, when Chris first had Spike, he took him everywhere with him, and this story is about one of the many 'incidents' that befell them on their travels...

This particular one occurred while Chris and three of his mates Gez, Zed & Zig (sounds like a circus group – of clowns!) were on their way to visit a friend in Blackpool. The four of them, and Spike, had got on the train in Birmingham, but can you believe it – they all forgot to buy a ticket!!! (ha ha, I know another one about three bears – that's a good fairy tale too!) It appears they *thought* they'd got away with it, until a ticket inspector came along to check the tickets.

Seeing the inspector meant this would mean trouble, so they set about trying to come up with a good excuse. After a few minutes contemplating, they realised they were in it up to their earholes, unless…

It was at this minute when Ziggy had a brainwave! (I use the term loosely, as that would imply the presence of a brain – and I don't think they had on between them!)

They decided to hide in the loo. Really? Spiffing idea chaps, I bet the ticket inspector would never *dream* of looking in there!!

Anyway, off they went, four rather tall lads, and one Staffy in search of a toilet to hide in. Mission accomplished, they waited for the ticket collector to work his way past them and tried to keep quiet. After a while, with no sight nor sound of the inspector, they decided he'd probably finished checking the tickets, and gone back to the other end of the train. Gez peeked through the door and saw the inspector was standing with his back to the sliding door of the next carriage. It wasn't safe to go out yet.

Having been confined in a small space for quite a while, they were all eager to get out, but knew they had to wait a little longer. They heard the guard asking for tickets again and then seconds later, they heard the carriage door slide open, as he came through into the area where the toilet was. They all held their breath as he seemed to walk past. Thinking they'd got away with it, they heaved a collective sigh of relief.

Just then, the guard knocked on the door, and Spike started barking. Game over!

"Would you like to come out of there please?" he asked

"Not really mate" answered Chris "I'm a bit busy!"

"No problem," the guard responded. "I can wait!"

They knew it was over – their goose wasn't just cooked; it was totally incinerated! They were just going to have to bite the bullet and face the consequences. Opening the door was a challenge, but once done, Spike led the way, and they trooped out one by one.

Seems the guard couldn't quite believe his eyes when the

door opened, and four beefy blokes and the Snitching Staffy came out of the loo!

"Well lads, I've seen some things in my time, but I have to say, this not only takes the biscuit, it takes the whole bloody packet! I almost jumped out of my skin when the dog barked – that was the last thing I was expecting to hear. How on earth did you all manage to get in there. I've never seen anything like it" the inspector said

Thinking the inspector was giving them some sort of accolade for their achievement, Zed, who was standing at the back piped up "Oh, it was easy really – we've done it before, but we didn't have Spike with us that time!"

"Is that so?" asked the inspector "and I suppose this is Spike?"

He bent down to stroke Spike, who was lapping up all the attention, and making quite a fuss of the inspector. Realising he seemed to like Spike, Chris decided to try and lighten the situation with a little humour.

"I could tell you the version about my dog wanting a drink, and bringing him to get a drink out of the sink, then spotting you, and then realising we'd forgotten to buy tickets, or…I could just tell you the truth and appeal for leniency"

"Now that will depend on whether your truth is fact or fiction, and whether I choose to accept it." said the guard "I'm looking forward to hearing all about how four, sorry five of you ended up in the loo so the dog could have a drink from the sink. How on earth can your dog drink out of the sink?"

"Just you watch…" sniggered Chris

With that, he uttered one of Spike's magic words.

"TAP – where's the tap Spike – have it!"

Tapped!

Spike dived back into the tiny confines of the lavatory, jumped on top of the loo, leaned over, and proceeded to bite the tap. Realising there was no water forthcoming, he changed tactics to the death stare. He could do death stare for hours if water was involved, but not today – they were in enough trouble, without having to recompense British Rail for a new tap!

The inspector couldn't help but laugh

"Well then, just when you think you've seen it all..." he grinned

With that, the lads started laughing, playfully asking Spike if he could lend them money for their tickets! After the short interlude, the inspector's face turned serious again.

"You know that travelling without a ticket is a serious offence and punishable with a fine. I should put you off at the next stop, but lucky for you, there isn't one - the train terminates at the next stop."

"What a stroke of luck that is then" laughed Zig, "so are we all going to be fined?" he asked

"Oh no, not all of you – Spike is actually travelling legitimately. He doesn't need a ticket!" affirmed the inspector.

"Where are you clowns and the performing dog travelling to anyway?" he asked

"We're going to have a few days by the sea and visit one of our mates in Blackpool. Donkeys, rock, kiss me quick hats and the Pleasure Beach!" Chris replied

"Blackpool!" exclaimed the inspector "Oh it really isn't your day is it?

With that, he left the lads between the two carriages, and went off in search of more tickets, leaving the bewildered lads to mull over what he'd said.

They stood trying to figure out exactly what the Inspector had meant. After a while he was back. The lads nodded sheepishly at him, as he bent to pat Spike.

"Well Spike, you're in a bit of a pickle aren't you lad. Not buying a ticket wasn't the only mistake these jokers made - they forgot to check where the train was going too. Not only is it the wrong train, it's travelling south- not north!"

"But we're going to Blackpool though" insisted Zed

"Not on this train you're not, and unfortunately, the next stop is London" the Inspector informed them, treating himself to a laugh at their predicament

"So, does it go to Blackpool after?" posed Zed

The inspector looked at him almost pitifully, before replying

"No lad, it terminates at London – that's the end of the line"

This news threw the lads into a quandary. How on earth had they managed to get on the wrong train, and worse still, how were they going to get to Blackpool?

Fortunately, the inspector took pity on the four rouges.

"I suspect" he said, "that you didn't check which was the correct platform for you."

"Yeah we did" piped up Zed

"So, you'll know there can be two different destinations from the same platform, depending if it's A or B?" the guard posed

"Eh? Well that's a bit daft isn't it? How do they expect people to get on the right train if there's two there? That's a bit too clever" complained Zed

"Well, you just listen to the announcement, ask one of the staff or read the timetable. The system works perfectly well, it's not rocket science, but obviously a bit too complicated for you dimwits!' replied the guard

"Yeah but it didn't work for us - we managed to get the wrong train" grumbled Zed

"I rest my case" laughed the guard

"Now then Spike, listen very carefully…" the guard went on "I think you lot are going to have enough problems getting to Blackpool without being fined as well. So, I've decided to forget I ever saw you on this train, and hopefully, be able to erase the experience from my mind without therapy! Everyone deserves a second chance, so perhaps in the future, you'll make sure they think twice before boarding a train without a ticket, but for now, poetic justice has been served!"

This brightened them up no end, and even though they neither knew, nor cared what poetic justice meant, they all had a laugh at their stupidity, commended the guard on his decision, and responded with articulate variations of thank you.

"Cheers mate"

"Diamond geezer"

"Ta pal"

"Nice one"

And other such eloquent expressions of appreciation and gratitude.

With London approaching fast, they made their way to the door in readiness to get off. As they waited, the guard went and stood beside them. Chris asked him,

"Did you know we were in the loo before Spike barked?"

"Oh yes" came his reply

"How?" Chris inquired

"One of you dozy buggers locked the door!

They all looked at Ziggy, who admitted he thought it would look better with the door locked.

Marks for ingenuity – Zero!

When the train entered London, four subdued, disheartened lads and one snitching Staffy descended to the platform. The inspector saw them walking away and shouted-

"Good luck getting to Blackpool lads, any idea how you're going to get there?" '

Zed turned around, and hollered

"Aye, no problems mate – we're getting the next train!"

Quite a quirky remark, from the lad who had once thought that 'Top Gear', was a particularly good batch of wacky backy!

And with that, they disappeared into the hustle and bustle of Euston station!

When the story was over, I asked him what, if anything he'd learned from the experience. Thinking he would say, not to travel without buying a ticket, I couldn't help but smile, when he said

"Don't take Spike the next time!'

The brains of the gang insisted on anonymity leaving the train.

MOVING MEMORIES

After refilling our glasses and grazing on nibbles, we moved on to when Spike first came to live with us. We'd gone past eating now, so I loaded up the nibbles again. I thought back fondly to the first time he came to stay with us – it seemed like only yesterday...

Chris had said he liked a ball, so we bought a couple for him. A large plastic one and a smaller tennis type one for when we took him out. We stood in the garden with him, and although he was eager to see what I had in my hand, the enthusiasm ended there.

I threw the ball to him – it hit him straight in the face, but he didn't seem to care, he just sat there staring at me. I tried to enthuse about the ball, but there was no reaction. I threw it again, and again it hit him (gently mind!) on the snout. No response whatsoever, just his head cocked to one side, with this blank, glazed stare as if to say, why are you throwing that thing at me? Am I meant to do something? Give us a clue! The ball lived to be thrown another day, and many more after that. He never did grasp the concept of 'fetch!'

There was another comical tale we remembered about the time he had a cow leg!

Many years ago, when we were 'caretaking' Spike, and BJ (before Jake) Chris turned up at our house with this enormous bone for Spike, saying a mate who was a butcher had given it to him for the dog. I had never seen a bone that big in my life – apart from on the t.v! Spike eyed it up and gave it a good sniffing, before deciding it was acceptable.

He dragged it down the garden and settled down for a good chew. He had never been a dog who growled when anyone went near his food, but this bone was a bit special, so he wasn't taking any chances, after all, any one of us might have fancied a chew or a lick of it! We didn't know if his good-natured dining habits extended to a big, juicy bone – and none of us were prepared to volunteer to find out!

It was his, and he didn't want anyone interfering in his business as he savoured the huge bone that looked to be almost as long as he was!

Well, he lay there for hours with his new best friend (the bone) to the point where he became obsessed with it. He didn't even want to come in for his dinner, which was unheard of for him! We tried to entice him inside, but he completely ignored us – he only had eyes for the bone, so we could do no more than to leave him to it.

As darkness began to fall, we were sure he'd come running, but no amount of calling or chivvying could persuade him to leave the beloved bone. He was going to have to leave it sooner or later, because bedtime was fast approaching, and we couldn't leave him out all night – could we? It was starting to look like we may have to.

Happily, Mother Nature intervened on our behalf and it started to rain. Gentle, little drops to begin with, but within minutes it was precipitating fairly heavily. Now for as much as Spike loved taps, baths and all things water, he wasn't too keen on being out in the rain, and realising him and the bone were getting wet, he decided to come indoors. Easier said than done, but he picked up the bone and came towards the door.

I told him, in no uncertain terms, there was no way he was bringing that bone indoors. He completely ignored me and tried to thrust himself and the bone through the door. Being so huge, there was no way it was going to come through the door sideways, but he wasn't going to let a little thing like size deter him, oh no, he kept pushing and shoving, but to no avail.

I know we shouldn't laugh, but we did. We stood and howled with laughter as this crazy mutt tried to get through the door with his monster bone! Then, he changed tactics. He dropped it (briefly) came into the conservatory, and began to pull it, but still it wasn't budging. Sooner or later he would realise that he would have to turn it around – surely?

Although Spike was a quite a clever little chap, his navigational skills amounted to zero and he's about as graceful as a house brick! He just wasn't blessed with ingenuity; unless, of course, water was involved, then it was just best to get out of his way, otherwise, you'd get 'snouted'!

He went back outside for another try, but the bone was not for turning! Finally, after everything else had failed, we resorted to Spikes 'Get out of trouble' card; the tap! Taps and shiny things override everything in Spike's world.

"Spikey, come and see the TAPS in the BATH!" I shouted, his two favourite words. Hesitant at first, but eventually unable to resist the allure, he abandoned the bone and came tearing in through the living room, into the hall, and biffed open the bathroom door! None of us were quick enough to get to the bathroom before him, so he jumped in the bath and did his 'stare' at the taps routine.

The glazed look that appeared on his face during the tap stare, was a sight to behold. The faraway expression together with his head cocked to one side, gave the impression he was trying to communicate with something or someone. The Mother Ship on some distant, far away planet perhaps?

Spike to Mother Ship... Come in Mother Ship...

No amount of shouting, promises, hand waving or any other form of gesticulation could divert his concentration. Only when the tap was turned on, and his jaws were snapping at the flow did the stare disappear. I'd love to know what was going through his mind – apart from all the tumbleweed that is!

Iain went out to hide the bone while Spike was busy trying to kill the tap, and things were quiet for the rest of the evening, but bedtime was a different story!

When he went out for his bedtime constitutional, he was looking for the bone. Didn't take him too long to find it, however, there was the small problem of a shed door standing between him and the new love in his life. I hate to ruin his street cred, but he snorted and howled for that bone, but eventually and very reluctantly, he came inside the house.

We let him have it again the following day, and he continued on his mission to eat it, but even his powerful jaws were no match for 'the bone' He spent hours out there giving it a good seeing to, he was addicted to it – like a canine form of catnip. We put it in the shed at night, so as not to attract any other visitors.

A couple of weeks later, we were getting ready to go shopping. Living in a rural area, a trip to the shops can take a few hours, so when we knew we would be gone a long time, we would lock the back gate, and leave the conservatory door open for him. That way, there would be no puddles, no need to restrict the time we were out, and definitely no burglars! No-one in their right mind would want to land in those jaws after scaling a six-foot six gate!

Stamford was our destination that day, so we'd only be away two hours – three tops. When we got back, we could see Spike's silhouette through the trellis at the bottom of the garden, his big, white head bobbing about, he didn't want to come down to us, so we began to pack away the food stuff. We always brought him a chew home when we'd been shopping, no doubt he'd be in looking for it soon. Iain went outside to put some things in the shed. but when he came back, he was bursting to tell me something.

"you're not going to believe this, but come and look at the shed door, you won't believe what he's done!" he sniggered

"He, being the one with four legs?" I asked.

I followed him down the garden towards the shed at the bottom. I had to laugh when I saw what had happened. Having tracked his beloved bone to the garden shed, he had taken matters into his own paws and set about freeing it. A hole had appeared in the shed door, and part of the cherished bone was poking through. The little devil had gnawed, pawed and crunched a hole in the wooden door, just big enough to get his paw through and pull the bone towards him. He didn't need it to be any bigger, he was quite content to lie there and lick the part he'd managed to pull out.

Later that night when we were putting the bone to bed, I noticed it was getting noticeably ripe, mind you, he'd had it a few weeks so no wonder it was minging! There was no way I was going to touch it, so Iain moved it with the help of an old supermarket bag. The bone was on its last legs – if you'll pardon the pun!

The following day, we decided the bone would have to go. I couldn't help wondering what the binmen would think if they noticed it - would they take it?

Iain said he would tell them it was all that was left of the last chap who refused to empty the bin! So as not to upset him, I took Spike for a walk while Iain disposed of the bone. When we got back, Spike went straight out to the back garden and started jumping up at the bin. Time for plan B...

Even though there were no flies on the little lad, it wouldn't be long before flies would be after his bone – it was rancid!

The only way to make things easier for Spike was to dispose of the bone away from the house, at the local tip. Hopefully, no-one would notice what was in the black bin liner, but if the police came knocking on the door with a warrant to search the garden, we'd know we were in trouble!

"That's not too bad an idea, the lawn could do with a good turning over!" laughed Iain. After discussing the matter, we decided that the local tip was a no-go for the bone, so we hid it in the roof of the garage until bin day. Once the dust cart arrived on our street, I put Spike upstairs, got the bone and threw it in the bin.

When he came down, he went and had a quick look around outside. He went to the shed, had a good sniff and then went to the garage. His huge snout working overtime, as this had been the bones final resting place! Finally, I think he realised his cherished prize had gone, so he came in the house and disappeared upstairs. The next time he went in the garden, there was no frantic searching for his treasure, so thankfully, things were back to normal. For a little while at least! My only regret is that none of us thought to take a picture of that dammed bone!! That would have been one for the family album for sure!

Where's mi bone?

Darkness had descended on our little house in more ways than one, but we were all eager to carry on talking about our crazy boy amid laughter and tears, Iain topped up the glasses and carried on talking. Thinking about when we first met him, brought another comical incident to mind…

I had taken him up to the fields for a good run, but Spike, being Spike, was very easily distracted, and after a couple of minutes running, he had a 'squirrel' moment, and went off at a tangent. Never one to acknowledge defeat, and stubborn as a mule - even when the object was much bigger than him, he would drag, pull and tug his prey, whatever it may be, until his mission was achieved, and the said object was firmly between his jaws.

Today's specimen – a huge log, (the size of a small tree!) was going nowhere and causing him a few problems – as in he couldn't move it. Not one to be put off easily, he got stuck in and pulled at the log, but to no avail. He wasn't a quitter so there he stayed - teeth firmly planted into the log, tense and determined to kill it! I walked off and left him grunting and groaning at it. He would catch up with me when he got fed up with it!

As I arrived at the next field, I could hear him barking in the distance; he was probably shouting to persuade it to move, but he would go home disappointed today, as the log was staying put! After a while, I shouted him, but as usual, he completely ignored me. So, I waited, waited some more, then got a chewy from my pocket and went back to retrieve him, but I was in for a shock when I saw the state of him!

His face was covered with blood, made to look worse against his white face, but it was his eyes that had me worried. They were very bloodshot and literally bulging out of their sockets. He looked a right sight!

"Oh my God Spike, what on earth is the matter boy? What have you done?!"

All sorts of scenarios went through my mind. Was he sick? Was there something on the log that was poisonous? Was he having some kind of attack? I felt sick with worry. I grabbed my mobile, found the vet's number and pressed the button. I put his lead on, and having ascertained his legs were ok, started running towards home.

When my call was answered, I told the lady on the other end there was something very wrong with my dog. I explained the bulging eyes and how worried I was. She asked if it was Spike, then told me to bring him down immediately – I didn't need telling twice!

We were home within a few minutes. I quickly grabbed the car keys, got him into the car, and set off on the four-mile journey to the vets. Once there, we jumped out of the car and rushed into reception and headed straight for the desk.

"Hello, this is Spike, I spoke to you about him a few minutes ago"

The receptionist gave me a quizzical look and said

"I don't think it was me you spoke to, let me just check. What did you say his name was?"

"Spike, he's got bulging eyes" I replied.

She looked down at her computer but couldn't find Spike or any evidence of a phone call. I was perplexed. Why couldn't she find us?

"I rang about twenty, thirty minutes ago, and the lady I spoke to told me to bring him down right away"

"I'm really sorry, I just can't find you. Let me just check with one of my colleagues. Take a seat for a minute and I'll sort this out"

While we waited, I stroked Spikes huge head, and tried to look at his eyes. Ever helpful, he turned his back on me and refused to let me look!

A few minutes later, the receptionist came over to us, and said there was definitely no indication of our call.

"Well I jolly well spoke to someone!" I protested, "I just don't understand what could have happened. Well, seeing as how I'm here now, can someone please take a look at him?"

"I'll see if anyone's available, I won't be a minute"

At this point, I started chatting to an old lady who was there with her cat in its little travelling basket. Spike was busy with his head under my seat, staring at absolutely nothing! I started telling her about my predicament, and she offered a couple of possible causes of the bulging eyes – both of which I'd considered.

Suddenly, one of the vets came out, and called for Spike. I pulled him from under the chair and walked into his examination room.

"So, this is Spike then, hello little man, what have you been up to?"

I love it when the vet talks to the animal, but me being me, I always think about 'what if?' – you know what I'm like! What a shock he would get if Spike answered him!

It may go something like…

"Eh well, I took her out for a walk up the fields, and let her go, you know, just to stretch her legs a bit. Anyway, I spotted this cracking tree branch, massive it was, just begging to be chewed. Well, I had to have a go – like you do! There I was, enjoying myself, and over *she* comes and starts interfering! You can't ignore her when she starts! Making all these weird noises she was, then she gets out that thing she always has in her pocket, and started talking to it, then, before I could say 'tap' she had that lead thing round my neck, and we were off and away. Ran me all the way home she did, my feet were fair killing me when we got back!

Next thing I know, I'm in the car on my way here. So, in reply to your question, I haven't got a clue!"

There I go, deviating from the story again – I just can't help myself!

Meanwhile, back in the real world…

I began relating why I had brought Spike to see him. Story finished, he picked Spike up and put him on the examining table. He turned Spikes head this way and that, and asked me,

"So, what did you say was wrong with his eyes? They look fine to me'

I went and stood in front of the dog and looked at him. I was both amazed and confused. Apart from his blood-stained face, he looked completely normal.

'What the hell!! I swear to you, they were bulging out of his head, I was worried to death, I thought he'd swallowed something he shouldn't have!'

'Do you know what I think has happened' offered the young vet 'You said he was biting vigorously on a tree branch when you noticed it. I think his eyes bulged because he was biting so intensely, I've seen it happen before, but I can understand why you were so worried, it can look kind of scary! Staffys' jaws are so powerful, and sometimes they bite so hard, it can make this happen. I'll check his eyes anyway, but I'm sure they'll be fine. I think the blood is from his tongue, looks like he's given it a good bite!

That had to be the explanation – little devil had bitten the branch so hard; his eyes had literally popped out of his head. Surely it must have hurt him. Staffys' seem to see pain as an occupational hazard!

With that, he proceeded to examine Spikes eyes. As predicted, he could find nothing amiss, and pronounced him fit and healthy. I thanked him for humouring me and left him in peace. Fit and healthy or not, there was still the small matter of the consultation fee to be paid, so I went back to the receptionist.

"He's okay then?" she asked

"Yes, he's fine, but I promise you, they really were bulging, and I really did make an appointment with somebody on the phone!"

"I was thinking about that; do you have the number that you rang?" she asked

"Yes, it's here on my phone"

I whipped that phone out of my pocket, quicker than Paul Newman's gun in Butch Cassidy! I scrolled down the contacts till I'd found the number.

"There you go" I showed her

'Mmmm" she sighed, "I'm afraid this isn't our number"

"Have you changed it?" I queried

"No, it's always been the same, but I think I know what might have happened. This is the number of the vets in town, you must have called them by mistake"

I pondered this for a few moments...

"Oh my God!" I squirmed "I must have done – I bet they're wondering where we are! I'll have to call and apologise when I get home. I'm so glad you solved the riddle; I was beginning to think I was losing my mind! I am so very sorry"

(I DO hope you're not laughing!)

I paid the fee, thanked them for being understanding, and beat a hasty retreat back to the car.

What an idiot!! I knew exactly what I'd done...

We were registered with different practise when we had Mr. Wigs, however, when Meathead came, we decided to use the new Veterinary Hospital on the outskirts of town – unfortunately, I hadn't changed the number! Muppet!

What threw me, was when I'd made the call, the lady I spoke to asked if it was for Spike, and I'd said yes, except, the Spike *she* was referring to was Mr. Wigs – our beautiful Golden Labrador, who left us several years before.

What a spectacular faux par! Iain dined out on that for weeks after!

I am a complete and utter goofball sometimes! Only I could do that!

All the reminiscing brought tears of both happiness and sadness. There were so many things Spike had done in his lifetime; it would take all night to recall and relate. Marcia hadn't known the little man too long but was more than happy to let us take over her special day with our memories of him.

Iain was next to recall an incident. This came about when a doctor called many years ago...

Due to problems with my back, I found myself in need of a home visit from my GP. Unbeknown to me my GP was away, so they were going to send a locum. Late afternoon, the phone rang and the voice on the other end said, "Oh hello, it's Dr. Johnstone, I've come to examine you" Thinking he was lost, which happens quite often to people trying to find our house, I asked him where he was?

"I'm at your front gate" he replied.

Somewhat puzzled, I asked, "Well are you going to come in? I don't much fancy being examined in the front garden!"

"I'm sorry, but I can't come in till I know that Staffy is locked up!" he said

"Sorry?" I replied "What do you mean locked up? Are you afraid of dogs?"

"Not all dogs, but I'm not too keen on those Staffy dogs, and the sign on your gate has me worried. I cannot come in until I know I'll be safe" he finished. The little sign on the front gate said; Beware of The Staffy. What it didn't say was 'because it will probably lick you to death'!

Luckily, Iain was home at the time, so he took Spike into the back garden, closed the doors and gave him a chewy. He then went to open the front door, and beckoned the doctor to come in.

He was very hesitant, and Iain had to convince him that it was completely safe, the dog was locked in the garden and had never, ever bitten anyone!

Tentatively, he came in and through to the living room. Anxiously, he tried to ask me about my pain, but he wasn't looking at me, he was looking through the French Windows at Spike, who by this time had eaten his chew, and was busy jumping up at the French doors. He had detected a stranger in his house with his mum – and he didn't like it one little bit! I must admit, he did look rather scary jumping up and sliding down the door, which was now covered in Staffy snot and saliva!

Trying to lighten the situation, I said "It's quite safe he's been fed, he doesn't bite, and he doesn't have a key!"

Poor choice of words. After that, there was no going back; the poor guy couldn't concentrate. I asked if he would be happier in my bedroom, but he said no, he wanted to keep his eye on the dog. I had tried to lighten the mood but failed spectacularly!

Well, as you might have guessed, I didn't get examined that day, and had to wait until I was well enough to go to the surgery! I know we shouldn't laugh at someone's misfortune, and we weren't really, it was watching Spike sliding down the patio door that set us off!

Ah bless you Spike, you've left us with such wonderful, funny memories...

The raw emotion of that day, and the stroll down memory lane had left us all feeling drained, but thankfully, we'd been able to share our grief as a family. To be with people we love, who loved him as much as we did made all the difference.

We always said that Spike would only go when he was good and ready, and he was ready that day. The little lad saved us the anguish of having to make that upsetting, most heart-breaking of decisions to assist him on his journey to the Rainbow Bridge, and for that we are incredibly thankful.

Before we leave Spike, there's one little thing I'd like to say.

I truly believe that little guy waited to say goodbye to us the day he died. We literally hadn't been in the house five minutes when he closed his eyes; he hung on till we got back. No one will ever convince me otherwise.

Of all the words I could use to describe him, (and believe me -there's quite a few!) there is just one that encompasses him completely and makes me smile whenever I hear it.

'Spiiiiike!'

No caption required...

'DISCO DOG AND DIRTY DANCING!

Everyone was down in the dumps the day after. We were all suffering from PSS (post Spike syndrome) it was such an empty feeling. Both Iain and Terry had gone to work, and Marcia was upstairs on-line, teaching English to Japanese students. She's a very resourceful girl, and a very good teacher!

Downstairs, I noticed Spike's bed had gone, no doubt Iain moved it to save my tears. There was, however, another little chap that needed some attention – Louie. His bed, in the opposite corner to where Spike's had been was empty, as he'd stayed in bed that morning – mine, not his! I poured some chow into his bowl, called him down and within seconds he was there.

"Right then Louie, just you and me from now on. We'll soon get our act together" he cocked his head to one side listening to what I was saying. He always did that, it was so endearing, and made him look so cute. However, he wasn't interested in cuteness, there were more, important things he ought to be attending to – breakfast being the top of his list. He was still finding his paws but felt it would be easier now. His tail had found it's wag and he'd started playing with us.

Unlike Spike, this little guy *loves* a ball, and never tires of playing fetch. He loves squeaky toys too, but they never last too long. De-squeaking, followed by dissecting/disembowelling is his preferred method of disposal, it was funny to watch! He could rip them to bits in minutes! Anything he gets - he has to kill.

We were back to Staffy-proof toys again, or rather the pursuit of them. Our efforts to find truly Staffy proof toys usually cost us a fortune, only to end up in the dustbin. I've only found one thing that my Staffies can't destroy easily, and that's coconuts. Doesn't stop them entirely but slows down the assassination process! I decided to try the idea a few years ago. If you shave all the hair from the outside, then pierce it to remove the milk, (although I leave a drop of it inside) it lasts for many days, it's cheap and safe. I'm not saying it's been tested or recommended by vets you understand? But it does the trick for my dogs. Best to give it to them outdoors though, just in case there's any milk left inside.

So now, it was Louie's time and like Spike before him, I knew this daft dog would help us through the following months, would help to heal ours heart...

One of the most remarkable things we discovered about him in those early weeks is the height he can jump. He managed to get out of the back garden one day, and we both accused each other of not shutting the gate properly. This Mancunian mutt sees every door/gate as a challenge, so we forgot about it – until he did it again. We devised a way to find out how he did it, although we both had our suspicions, they seemed unlikely. I went and stood in the street outside and shouted him. Within seconds, a pair of paws appeared on top of the gate, followed by a head, then finally the rest of him. He threw himself over the top, landed right beside me, wagging his tail, waiting for applause!

"Oh my God, I thought climbing over was a possibility, but assumed it more likely that he'd found a little hole in the hedge and forced his way out! Even with those lanky legs of his, I didn't really think he'd jump over it!" I gasped

The gate in question is six foot six, but him clearing it took our thoughts back to the puzzle of his parentage – could it be Skippy? (the bush kangaroo – an Australian television programme for children in the sixties)

Once back in the garden, he was eager to do it again and though it was funny to watch, I was concerned that he might hurt himself – even though *he* wasn't.

There was a time when we wondered if we should change his name to Houdini, as it seemed nothing could stop him getting out of the 'dog proof' garden if he wanted to. To this day, he is barred from going in the front garden, as the little gate poses no challenge at all to him, he could practically stride over it!

One evening a few months after we'd got him, he went on one of his excursions. After having jumped the gate previously, we were a bit dubious about leaving him unsupervised, he just wasn't to be trusted! Of course, he wasn't going to jump while we were watching him, he waited and seized his opportunity.

There was a knock on the front door and because Louie was in the back garden, I shut him out there while I went to answer the door. Before I could ascertain what the visitors wanted, I noticed this black streak by the front gate. It was him! The little devil had jumped the back gate and come around the front. He wasn't going to miss out on the chance to bark at visitors. He hopped over the gate, came up the path and while he was doing a low-level growl, he gave them a darn good sniffing. I was mortified! He is not the most obedient dog we've had.

Luckily, they were dog lovers too so didn't mind him giving them the once over. After the introductions had taken place, the callers went on to tell me they were collecting on behalf of the R.S.P.C.A.

Quick as a flash I pointed at Louie and said, "here – you can have this with pleasure!" They both smiled, a sort of pitiful smile that said, another owner that can't control their pet!

"Ah he's a lovely boy though aren't you Louie, even if you are a wee monkey" laughed the girl, "You know your mammy's

only kidding aren't you mammy?" Right at that moment –
mammy was deadly serious!

I smiled a somewhat contorted smile as Louie continued to
fuss and sniff them. There was no way he was going to behave
himself, so I told them I'd better get the 'wee monkey' back
inside and settle him down. It wouldn't do to tell representatives
of the R.S.P.C.A that I was going to take him in and batter him!
(not that I would of course – just a figure of speech!)

Wee monkey, my elbow - if only they could hear what my
mind was calling him – it sure as hell wasn't little monkey! It
begins with little, but I assure you, second word isn't monkey!

Little 'Monkey'

There were many things we'd yet to find out about this lad
(fur baby just doesn't do it for this adolescent fur kid) He had his
own ideas but training him was an uphill battle. He wasn't
naughty as such, he would do as we asked, but once he'd done it
– that was your lot! Getting him to 'stay' was impossible unless
we stayed too. He would 'sit' but again, his bum was off the
floor as soon as I'd turned away.

He was never going to win any accolades for obedience!

Things were not getting better at bedtimes either because of his nocturnal antics. Every night we had to endure his bed bopping frolics! I tried going in the spare room, but it didn't work because he could (and did) open the door. He would split his time between the two rooms, disturb both of us, and would howl if he couldn't get in! Because Iain had to go to work, he usually stayed with me. Although he would stay on the floor, he was up on the bed the minute he felt he could, and for me, the bounce on the bed was enough to wake me. Not Iain though – he can sleep through anything.

Had I stayed in my own bed, not only would I have Louie doing his Strictly (come dancing) routine every night, I'd have had Iain providing the soundtrack too, and had no peace whatsoever!

Unfortunately, it was a long time before were able to reclaim our bed!

GRENDEL

Trying to explain the logic of Grendel, is a bit like the offside rule in football; - I will try and explain it, but I doubt you'll understand!

When Chris first met Louie, he didn't think the name suited him and began spouting other names he thought to be more appropriate, one of which was Grendel, only he pronounces it as 'Greeeen- Deeel' l in a high pitch, squeaky voice which sends Louie into a frenzy.

For whatever reason, (or maybe because the dog is as daft as he is) Louie responded to this, so Chris decided that Grendel would be his pet name for him. The only thing is – Louie thinks that Chris is called Grendel too, which causes many a laugh, and much confusion for Louie! He answers to Grendel and looks for him at the same time. Perhaps he thinks that whenever he hears Greeen -Deeel, he's meant to do something, but what, well, he doesn't know – we certainly don't, so your guess is as good as ours! What I do know for sure, is we have, yet another dog with faulty wiring!

As the days passed our spirits lifted a little and we were beginning to come to terms with losing Spike. Like any passing, you learn to adapt and live with it – but you never truly get over it. Louie played a huge part in this, with his clowning around. Without Spike, the Mancunian Mongrel had found his paws, all four of them were well and truly under the table!

Quite a vocal little fella, he produces the strangest noises, and always has plenty to say about everything! It took us a while to figure out the difference between happy and snappy noises. Eventually, we discovered they are all the same, it's the volume that makes the difference. A low-level growl means he is not amused, but it's very rare we hear that one, mainly, they're happy noises. Getting him to shut up is another thing! This constant grumbling and mumbling earned him another nickname – Mr. Gobalot! He really makes his presence felt when he starts!

Seeing as how he loved playing with a ball so much, we gave him Jakes red ball. It's a hard, solid ball, and far too big for him to pick up, so he just biffs it everywhere. He makes an awful lot of noise and gets frustrated because it's too big to fit it in his jaws. Any passing stranger would think we were trying to kill him! On the other hand, his co-ordination is absolutely amazing! He could teach some of these footballers a thing or two!

Visions of Louie wearing the sky blue of Manchester City comes to mind. (Other clubs are available!) With those long, lanky legs of his he'd be this side, that side, onside, offside, inside, outside and everywhere in between! I can't resist imagining the scene. The commentary *could* go something like this: -

'City have brought on a substitute, a bit of home- grown talent here. Grendel, a new signing, we've not seen this lad before. Just LOOK at the speed he moves that ball, he's fast! Further up the field now, he's offside, no, wait a minute, he's onside. He's got the ball in his mouth now, is that the same as handball? He's not giving possession away, he's off like greased lightening, no-one else is getting a look in; this lad means business. One of the opposition goes in for a tackle, but Grendel glides past and he's off and away again. Heading down to the goalpost, and yes, he scores - both him and the ball are in the back of the net – it's a goal for Manchester City!

The goalkeeper has a fight on his hands to get the ball off him, but has a trick up his sleeve to distract him. He throws a chewy out into the field. It does the trick, as Grendel drops the ball and runs off. Now, the goalkeeper places the ball on the floor, and kicks it out. But what's this? Grendel's head appears above the heads of the other players; he's eaten the chewy, he intercepts the ball and he's off again. Where's he going now?

He's taking an unofficial corner, er, maybe he's not – *oh no*, he's cocked his leg up against the corner flag, and he's having a pee! The ref's holding up a yellow card, but he ignores it, and off he goes. He's racing towards the goal area, but what's he doing now? He's stopped... He seems to be circling; almost like he's looking for the right spot... seems he's found it too! He squats down, and *oh no* he's offloaded a present for the other team in the penalty area – that's what he thinks of the opposition! That will be a red card for sure – a definite foul if ever I saw one! Just when you think you've seen it all, along comes Grendel!

They think it's all over – it is now!"

(yes, I know – my wiring could need adjusting too!)

Like our other lads before him, he just *loves* a balloon, and won't rest till he kills it. One of the first times we gave him one, I put it in the hanging, flower basket holder, which hangs from the trellis above the decking – and just out of his reach. He tried his best to get to it, but he couldn't quite reach. He sat for a while, and then took a run at it, and tried climbing up the post in the middle! When that didn't work, he changed tactic. He jumped up on the table, and launched himself at it, and tried to grab it in mid-air, but still he couldn't get it.

He was getting desperate by now, and I was having visions of the trellis, the basket holder and everything else landing on his head, so thought it best to dispose of the balloon with a pin. The loud pop made him jump out of his fur, but he couldn't understand where it had gone. He spent the rest of the day looking for it. Poor Lou!

His energy never seems to diminish, he's up for everything every day, and no matter how we try, we never seem to be able to wear him out! I recollect one day, I'd taken him for a long walk in the morning, and took him again with Iain in the afternoon, thinking he would have no energy left to cause any trouble.

Our route took us past a wheat fields, and for whatever reason, Louie disappeared into it. We couldn't see him, but we could see where he was because the heads of the wheat were moving around, indicating his path of destruction!

I shouted him back, but he ignored me. Iain called him, and he ignored him too. There was nothing for it, I would have to turn up the volume!

'Louie, get out here now!' I shouted, and yet again, he ignored my request. We could see he was busy as the wheat kept on swaying. He was having a whale of a time in there! All of a sudden, a few yards in front of us, his head appeared on top of the wheat, closely followed by the rest of him. It was like he had spring-loaded legs and using all four of them at the same time to do vertical jumps! I can't tell you how funny it was. Well, we laughed, then laughed some more at this stupid dog. Luckily, I managed to get a photo of him before he gave up. He was covered in bits when he finally decided to come out.

Spring loaded legs!

The dog, like one of his predecessors, he has a short circuit in his brain – in other words – he's round the bend!!

Sadly, the time had come for Terry & Marcia to leave. Although in one way, it would be nice to have the house back, I was going to miss them terribly. We'd had some laughs, and a couple of tears during their stay, I would also miss Marcia's cooking – it was lovely to have someone else cook sometimes, and she was good! They needed to go and make some new memories of their own now, and it was with a heavy heart, and a few tears (well, ok – so there was lot of tears, but don't let on coz he'll laugh at me!) that we said goodbye...

THE FOOL WITH THE STOOL

Like thousands of other people throughout the world, I suffer from back pain, and like the rest of them, I often find it very difficult to get comfortable and stay that way for any length of time. I try to suffer in silence (Are you kidding me – I so don't!) and have been known to try out all manner of different things that purport to alleviate the pain. The only thing I haven't bought as yet, is magic beans!

Writing involves a lot of sitting, and despite many breaks, I find it hard to sit for any length of time. I'd fancied trying one of those Kneeling Stools, thinking that it would take the pressure off my back, thereby helping me to sit for longer.

It's two cushioned pads, set at an angle on a wooden frame - one being higher than the other. It's designed so that you sit on the higher of the two seats, and rest your knees on the lower one in front of you; thus, giving you the correct sitting position. It's meant to take the pressure off your back, by distributing the weight to your lower legs. It has wheels on it for ease of moving too. That's the theory anyway...

Having looked at them on various websites, I couldn't believe the variation in prices! They went from, 'that thing will fall to bits when my bum gets on it, to ouch, to are you serious?!'

The problem was, I didn't want to spend a fortune on one of these things, only for it to end up in the garage covered in cobwebs – along with the rest of my discarded 'must haves!'

Iain came to the rescue, by finding one for sale on Ebay that seemed to be just what we were looking for. It's almost like it was meant to be; not only was the seller in our area, and asking a reasonable price, but she lived on one of Iain's delivery routes in Leicester! (who was now semi-retired and doing a part-time delivery job for the prestigious Hambleton Bakery) After a quick phone call to her, she said we could pick it up the following day. Bingo!

Iain came home with it in the passenger seat of the van, I was so excited! He brought it inside and I gave it the once over. Louie was very interested in it too, but then he sticks his snout in anything new that comes through the door. It was everything she said it was, and was in immaculate condition, sadly, she just couldn't get on with it. I couldn't believe my luck; however, it wouldn't stay that way for long – the Kneeling Stools days were numbered!

During the next few weeks, me and the stool tried to get acquainted with each other. It felt weird at first, but I was determined this stool would be my salvation. I was trying to finish my first book (Fully Staffed) at the time and believed that I would be able to finish it and write one book a month after that! (ha ha!)

Because the weather was sunny and warm, I decided to do some writing in the garden, so I took the stool downstairs, and left it in the conservatory while I went back to collect the rest of my things. Louie was in there sitting by the windows, he loves to see what's going on outside. In fact, we refer to the front bedroom as 'Louie's Office', because if he's not with us, he'll be up there, stood on his chair by the window, keeping the road outside under surveillance! Heaven forbid another dog should walk past!

He put the chair there himself too! One day, Iain and me were in the bedroom watching something going on in the road outside. He was beside himself because he couldn't see, and because neither of us would pick him up to see, he dragged the chair across to the window and hopped on it. He's so cheeky!

Louie in his office

Anyway, when I went back to the conservatory that day, there was a sight to behold – I just hope I can describe how funny it was!

Louie had hold of the stool. He'd stuck his teeth into the lower pad, and I watched in total bewilderment as he dragged it around the conservatory. I yelled at him to leave it, but he took no notice whatsoever! It was one of those moments (My life has a lot of these!) where you shouldn't be laughing, but just can't help yourself! The dog's onboard computer system was malfunctioning, and I couldn't stop him for laughing!

Not content with dragging it around the conservatory, he dragged it to the door, and attempted to take it outside. This proved to be a huge dilemma! He didn't want to let go of his trophy, but he couldn't get through the door with the stool in his mouth, as only one of the French windows was open. I suppose you may wonder why I didn't open the other one to make it easier for him?

Don't be daft, I was having way too much fun to be sensible!

What I *did* do was to get my mobile and record him. No-one would believe this crazy story without evidence! I watched as he and the stool went round and round, backwards and forwards, trying to figure out the best course of action! This was one determined dog, and he was not going to let the stool beat him! Eventually, he biffed his way out, sunk his teeth deep into the cushion, and dragged it into the garden.

I followed in anticipation, desperate to see what he was going to do now he was out of the confines of the conservatory. Off they went, dancing down the garden, I could barely keep my mobile still for laughing! Halfway down the garden, he came to a stop; he'd finally run out of steam – but not for long.

The minute he saw me moving towards him, he put his two front paws over it. I guessed there was going to be a struggle to reclaim it, so l turned off my mobile, and went indoors for bribery chews! What happened next, well, let's just say I'm glad I'd stopped recording him, because there's no way I would have been able to show the video to my family and friends!

Having mentioned Louie's antics with the chair to my dear friend and brilliant author, Brian L Porter, he suggested I write a poem about it for his poetry competition. Being an obliging kind of lady, I did just that, and entered the competition. I was amazed to find out I'd won!

I must point out that it wasn't only Brian who judged the poems – wouldn't want you to think I'd had preferential treatment! Brian has helped me so much with my writing – it was he who gave me the confidence to submit my first manuscript, and I will always be grateful to him. After reading his book about the beautiful 'Sasha', one of his many rescue dogs, I was inspired to write and dedicate a poem to her, which he kindly published in his book 'Sheba – from hell to happiness' I was thrilled to bits!

Sadly, the kneeling stool didn't help as much as I'd hoped it would. You'll never guess where it is...

Here's the poem about the stool...

LOOPY LOU

I have a dog called Louie, a little Staffy Cross, but what that is
exactly, I'm really at a loss!
His legs are long and lanky, his paws so big and white, a pair of
ears just far too big, and a brain not wired up right!
He's clumsy and he's crazy, a proper Canine clown, his antics
keep me smiling, he's fun to be around.
His tails wags fast as lightening, I fear there'll come a day,
unable to control it, he'll wag himself away!
Although he's just adorable, he has some strange ideas, we never
know what's coming next, there's nothing this lad fears.
One balmy day last summer, he really was a fool, the master of
disaster took umbrage with my stool!
He dragged it to the garden, the poor stool came to grief, and
while he deconstructed it, I watched in disbelief!
I didn't know the reason, for Louie's deadly strike, was it simply
just the stool, or colour he didn't like?
Who knows what thoughts abound him, it's very strange
indeed, his brain is full of Candyfloss, and lots of
tumbleweed!
Though none of us are perfect, one thing I know for sure, this
dog brings out the best in me, his heart is true and pure.

He gives me so much pleasure, my loyal and faithful friend. I'll love this boy forever, even though he's round the bend!

The nut job!

TIA'S TALE

Mid- September 2013, I had a phone call from Nicky – nothing unusual about that, except today, she was telling me about her sister-in-law's quest to find a new home for one of her employees' dogs.

Sound familiar? It should do! I sort of knew what was coming, so listened intently as she told me all about a little girl called Tia.

'So anyway, the lady who has her is ever so upset' Nicky continued, 'she's asked everyone she can think of but had no luck. She doesn't want to give her to the dogs' home for fear of her being 'put to sleep' '

How I loathe those three words...

She went on to tell me that the dog was a black Staffy called Tia. (that clinched it!) She wasn't entirely sure of the reasons for her needing a new home - she wasn't vicious or anything, in fact, she was quite timid, and although her 'mum' loved her to bits, she just couldn't keep her anymore. Hearing she lived with a seven -year- old boy, told me she was probably good with children too.

'How old is she' I asked

'She's just two' came the reply. Spooky- Louie was 'just

two' too!

'Well, obviously I'll have to speak to Iain, but the main problem is whether she'll get on with Louie. He kind of likes having us all to himself, but he might be okay with a girlie dog.'

If Louie approached his new lady friend with the enthusiasm, he gave to everything else he did, we'd be over-run with puppies in no time at all, and I'd be ringing Nicky for a change!

'Leave it with me Nicky, and I'll get back to you as soon as I've spoken to Iain. If he's really dead against it, we'll see if we can arrange a home somewhere down here for her. He'll be back from work soon, so I'll ring you later. Tell the lady who owns her not to do anything just yet" and with that, I put the phone down – and started plotting, (sorry planning!) Tia's travel plans, and my gentle persuasion speech for when Iain came home. At least we wouldn't have to change her name like we had for Louie! Tia was a lovely name.

For those of you who haven't read Fully Staffed (my first book) we tease Nicky, our sister-in-law, by calling her – St. Nicola; international dog/cat rescuer, because she will rescue anything – even if it doesn't need rescuing! Her services are limited to Lancashire, Cheshire & Yorkshire these days, but recently, she bought a new car – with a big boot…

The minute Iain arrived home that day, he sensed something was afoot, and as soon as I mentioned that Nicky had phoned and told me a sorry tale, he said

'What sort, what colour, how old, male/female, is there any point of me saying no?' he asked.

'Staffy, black, two years two months, female - no!',

'I see, but don't forget, we've got Terry's wedding in November, so we'd have to leave her, and she might not have settled in by then'

He was right (yes, he can have that one!) I hadn't thought that far ahead. There had to be a solution, and you just know I wouldn't rest until I'd found it!

That evening, I rang Nicky and told her about our dilemma.

Like me, when it comes to animals, there are no problems – only solutions.

'So Iain didn't say no then?' she asked

'Oh no, we're just concerned about what we'd do with her when we go to the wedding. Chris will look after Louie, but I'm not sure it's a good idea to bring her down here, and then leave her so soon after. It's going to be a huge wrench for her as it is, without us leaving her so soon afterwards.'

Terry and Marcia were getting married early November, and the venue being in Thailand, meant we'd be away for a while.

At this point, Nicky came up with a possible way around it.

'I could always have her while you go to the wedding if it would help?' Mmmm that's a plausible idea that may work

'Let me sleep on it Nicky' I said, 'things might look different tomorrow – I'll get back to you. We can't keep this little girl waiting too long – nor her mum!'

Iain and I tried to think of a way to resolve the predicament but couldn't think of a way out without leaving her.

The next day things were looking a little brighter and brought about a possible solution. Thoughtful as it was that Nicky offered to have Tia, it didn't change the fact that she would be left. If anything, on reflection, it might be worse, as she'd have twice the disruption. No, we'd come up with another solution that was so simple, I don't know why I hadn't thought of it straight away!

I would ring Tia's mum, and explain our dilemma, and see if she could wait until we'd been to the wedding. After that, we would definitely take her providing Louie accepted her. If not, we had a very good Dogs' Trust in Leicester, and if we couldn't rehome her ourselves, we'd take her there. Job done!

I rang Nicky and told her what we'd decided. She was thrilled to bits with our plan. We decided that Nicky should pass on our phone number and ask Tia's mum to ring us. I somehow felt that if she wasn't really genuine, she wouldn't call – I needn't have worried, she rang within minutes of getting the number.

Tia's mum was a lovely young lady called Lee, who lived in Yorkshire with her son Lennon, who was seven at the time. I could tell within minutes, that this young lady was 100% genuine, and the decision to part with her beloved baby girl was breaking her heart. Sadly, due to a change in her circumstances, she could no longer keep Tia – it wouldn't be right. She'd had Tia from a few months old, so it hadn't been easy for her to make the decision to rehome her.

After a long conversation (a very long conversation – in which Lee gave me a severe listening to) we agreed that Tia would stay where she was until we came back from the wedding. I think it helped Lee to feel better about the situation, knowing that she wouldn't be going to a dog shelter. Also, when she drove her down, she would get to see where Tia would be living, meet Louie, and spend a little time with her new family. I gave her the dates we'd be away and told her I would ring to make necessary arrangements when we were back. Another fur baby – YEAH!!!!

A very shy Tia Maria

THAILAND HERE WE COME!

We flew out for the wedding as planned. My sister Beverley and her husband Michael were also going to the wedding and the four of us were looking forward to meeting everyone, and having a good time. It was going to be quite a trek to get there, three flights, and a boat trip!

The first bit was relatively easy – Manchester to Heathrow, then Air Malaysia for around thirteen hours to Kuala Lumpur. Once there, we'd change to Bangkok Airlines for another flight down to Koh Samui. The final bit of our journey was by ferry to Koh Phangan, which should take around 25/30 minutes, culminating with a forty-minute drive to the hotel.

Sometime the day after we'd left Manchester, four bedraggled, tired individuals arrived at Kuala Lumpur airport. We had a couple of hours to wait for our connecting flight, which gave us plenty of time to stretch our legs and have a drink. While Beverley and I had a mooch round the shops, Michael & Iain decided they would find out where our departure gate was. Although our luggage had been checked straight through to Koh Samui at Manchester, Michael decided to go and confirm this. How glad we were he did!!

When he came back and told us it had been lost, we thought he was kidding us, and seeing as how none of us were in the mood for a joke, we threatened to kill him if he didn't stop messing! Sadly, he wasn't messing – our luggage had gone off on a journey of its own.

Just then, a young man from the airport staff came over to explain the situation. They hadn't really lost all our luggage; they knew exactly where it was; it was en-route to Bangkok! He seemed to think this little update would somehow, make us feel better. Wrong! This information was just enough to tip my little sister's normally calm demeanour from sweet to psycho! I opened my mouth to speak, but it was Beverley's voice that came out!

"Bangkok! Are you *KIDDING* me? Why the hell is it going to Bangkok?!" She went on to tell the bearer of this bad news, in no uncertain terms, she would *NOT* be leaving without her luggage, so best they get it back, and sharpish! Didn't they know we were on our way to a wedding, which was in two days' time!

Unbeknown to us, the staff at Kuala Lumpur were used to dealing with missing luggage – and hissy fits!

"It happens all the time" one of the staff members whispered to me

"Er, I wouldn't mention that to the lady over there" I said nodding towards Beverley "she might just rip your liver out the mood she's in!" Normally, I'm the one with the verbal's (only when I'm poked with a stick mind) when the occasion arises, so it was a change to watch instead. Go on Bev!

Meanwhile, the final call for our flight was announced. We were already at the gate; it was just a matter of getting our hand luggage through the scanner. Having been reassured again about our missing bags and told that there were no other flights to Koh Samui that day, Beverley reluctantly put her bag through the scanner. Her parting comment to the airport staff, was to remind them we'd be travelling back through the airport in a few days... and if she hadn't been reunited with her suitcase...

The flight to Kho Samui was smooth and uneventful. Once there, we even managed to find the ferry we needed without too much trouble. Just before we boarded, I rang Terry to let him know we'd landed, and told him about our luggage. I couldn't believe his reply.

It appeared Elaine, Marcia's mum had also lost her luggage – or rather the airline had. Can you believe it! So that was mother of the bride/parents of the groom and aunty and uncle – you couldn't make it up! No wonder they say God laughs when you make plans!

After a fairly smooth crossing, we disembarked at a very busy Koh Phangan, and all started looking for Terry, who was supposed to be meeting us, but there was no sign of him. I tried to call him, but there was no reply. Eventually, a young man who'd been standing to the side of us, asked if we were heading for Terry and Marcia's wedding. He was here to collect another guest for the wedding - heard us mention Terry and a wedding, so he offered us a lift to the hotel. We were so grateful. We climbed into the back of his Tuk Tuk, armed with what little luggage we had, and set off, along with the other guest, a beautiful, young Japanese lady, (whose name I forget – sorry!) on a somewhat bumpy drive to the hotel.

When the driver stopped, he pointed over his shoulder, and told us our hotel was 'just down there.' Just down there was one of the steepest pathways I have ever seen, it gave me touch of Vertigo just *looking* down it. Just as well we didn't have our suitcases with us, or they would have been there before us! All the little chalets on either side, belonged to the hotel. We all leaned backwards to walk down this monumental slope, and went in search of the elusive, lesser spotted Terry. However, within a few minutes, we heard his voice behind us.

"Biddy! Yo the Bid!" I'd know that voice I love anywhere.

God I couldn't wait to get my hands on him! After the customary hugs all round, he told us why he'd missed us at the port. Him and Marcia had been running a bit late, when they set off to the dock to meet us and got there just in time to see us driving past them in a Tuk Tuk! I think God was laughing again!

After we'd checked in, we were taken to our rooms to find a nice surprise waiting for us. Marcia, ever resourceful and practical had gone to a shop, along with another young lady, and bought some toiletries, tee shirts, shorts and flip-flops for us all. Bless her, so kind and thoughtful, we were all very grateful. We were so glad that our room was nearer sea level than those at the top of the slope, but Iain thought one at the top may have been better. His reasoning being, that him and Michael wouldn't be able to climb the hill after a few beers, so would have to stay in the bar!

I'm sure my husband has a Micky Mouse watch. It has no numbers, and every time the big finger gets to where 12 should be, it says Beer-O-Clock!

I'm pleased to say that the young man at Kuala Lumpur airport, was as good as his word, because the following evening, our luggage was delivered to our rooms.

The wedding took place on the beach; with the gentle sound of the waves whispering against the shore, the sun shining down, and lots of love in the air - it was a beautiful, happy day. I managed to stay relatively tear free too, which is unusual for me. Terry was still, and always will be my little boy, so to see him about to start on a new, exciting chapter of his life, was happy, tinged with a little sadness. The sadness because I knew he was going to make his home in Houston, so I wouldn't get to see him very often. I rarely saw him as it was, but at least we'd be able to look forward to visiting them in Texas.

The day ended where it had begun – on the beach, only this time, we all lit pretty, orange lanterns and after making a few wishes, we watched as silently, they rose into the dark night sky. Only when the very last one had disappeared did we go back inside.

A few days later, we returned to the U.K., and this time, there were no challenges along the way – quite boring really. I half expected an armed guard waiting to escort us through Kuala Lumpur airport, but everything went smoothly. Never underestimate the power of the 'hissy fit!' Tomorrow, we would be back in Rutland, and one step nearer to our new baby girl!

TIA TIME

Louie greeted us with sheer delight when we arrived home, almost knocking our legs from under us, I thought he was going to wet himself! I swear if he'd wagged that tail any harder, he would have taken off! Mind you, I guess he would have been glad to see anyone, after spending ten days with Christopher! (only kidding Chris!)

Lee rang us the following day before we'd had chance to call her. She needed to be sure we hadn't changed our minds – no, we hadn't, so we set about making plans to meet them. We arranged for her and Lennon to drive down that weekend. We both thought it wise we should meet on common ground to introduce the dogs, so Lee would ring us when she arrived outside our house. Iain would then walk Louie up to the sports field, and Lee, Lennon and me would walk up a different way.

Bang on time, Lee called to tell me they were outside, so while Iain took Louie off to the field, I went out to greet them.

A beautiful, slim, young lady with long, dark hair emerged from the car, followed by her son Lennon.

"Hello Lee, lovely to meet you at last" I smiled. It seemed such a long time since we had first spoken. Turning to the little boy I said, "and *you* must be Lennon!" He gave me a lovely, shy little smile and nodded his head. After the preliminary questions; how the journey was, how long did it take etc... she got Tia from the car and we went inside.

I fell in love with that little girl the minute I saw her. Oh she was a little beauty; all black, except for a white little toe at the back, and the flash of white on her chest, that most Staffies seem to have. She had the most beautiful big, brown eyes that melted my heart, but she looked so sad. Under the circumstances, I guess it was understandable. I bent down and whispered to her "hello beautiful little girl" Lee had brought her special cushion, blanket, feeding bowls, crate, collar, lead, toys – (all the accessories that a girlie dog needs) which we took into the kitchen. Tia didn't seem to be too interested in what we were doing and stayed close to Lee.

After I'd collected my coat, we all walked up to meet Iain. It was a fairly pleasant day, so I didn't need to load up the layers. As we walked along, Lee started to tell me all about Tia...

She was the 'runt' of the litter apparently, therefore had been at a disadvantage, and in constant competition with the rest of the litter, which had made the little girl very nervous – something that has stayed with her to this day.

Things had gone well to start with, but sadly, Lee and her husband had separated, which meant Tia was spending most of the daytime in her cage. Lee had to work. Poor little soul... I knew where Lee was coming from, and it was *because* of her love for Tia she had come to the decision to rehome her. Lennon was heartbroken too, Tia was his buddy, and he was very sad to part with her. Nevertheless, after Lee had explained all this to him, and told him he could come and see where and who she was going to live with, he was a little bit more accepting. He was a lovely little boy – a credit to his mum!

When we finally reached the field, I could see Iain and Louie playing ball in the distance. They soon spotted us, but before

Louie could run over to us, Iain put his lead on – better safe than sorry! Introductions over, we let the dogs check each other out. Louie was beside himself when he met Tia, his tail at warp speed wag - he was desperate to get to her. However, being somewhat fearful, Tia made it perfectly clear that she wasn't too keen on letting this strange dog push his snout where it wasn't wanted and sat down. We stood chatting, and eventually took off their leads. Louie being his usual, boisterous self was bouncing about all over the place, desperate for her to play with him, but Tia was having none of it, and remained by Lee's side – she didn't want to play.

I've often wondered if somehow, she knew what was happening, and was upset by the whole thing? They know far more than we give them credit for sometimes!

As it was getting colder, and no sign of Tia wanting to play, we made our way back to the house for a warming cup of tea and a piece of cake. Lennon had made a 'thank you' card for us; - 'Thank you for taking care of Tia' - almost had me in tears, particularly as I knew how much he didn't want to part with her! I still have it to this day… He had become a little more relaxed with us now, and we chatted away like old friends. I told him that him and his mum could come visit Tia ANY time they wanted to, and that Iain, me and Louie would take very, good care of her. He could send cards, letters anything he liked, he could phone too if he wanted, and I would send them photographs of Tia. This seemed to lift his spirits.

Then, Lee and Lennon's dreaded moment arrived – it was time for them to begin their long drive back to Yorkshire. I knew how hard this was going to be leaving their little girl behind, as we got to the door, Lee's eyes filled with tears – mine did too. They say it's better not to look back, but it's so hard not to. At the gate, I hugged her and Lennon, and reassured them that we would love and cherish Tia, and that she would want for nothing. We were only a phone call away. And, if during the next few weeks, they found it impossible to live without her, we would drive her back to them.

As I watched them drive away, I gave them a last wave, and went in to Tia. Then the tears came... this poor little soul looked absolutely terrified, but I knew it was best not to fuss her too much and let her come to me. My tears were for her. How was she feeling about all this? Why had Lee and Lennon gone and left her? Would they come back later? Who knows what was going through her mind?... Her eyes staring at the door, looking for Lee and Lennon. I wish I could have explained to her what was happening.

Iain suggested we put up her crate so she could see and smell something familiar and take refuge in it if she wanted to. She showed no interest- her eyes remained fixed on the door. Louie was still trying to persuade her to be his new BBF, but she totally ignored him. I offered her a little chewy, but she turned her nose up. It seemed the only thing she wanted, was to see Lee and Lennon walk back through the door. There was nothing we could do, except wait and do things on her terms...

After sitting beside her and talking softly for a while, she let me stroke her. I knew we were making progress, when she pawed me because I'd stopped! We gave her some dinner, but she only ate a few mouthfuls. We let her dictate the rest of the evening, and as the hours passed, she seemed happier to let Louie sit beside her. Now on his best behaviour, he seemed to know his new friend needed some space and didn't mither her too much.

At bedtime, we let Louie out for his final patrol of the perimeter, and Tia followed him. This was looking promising! When they came back, we tried to get her to go in her little crate, but she refused. Mindful that Louie had spent most of his nights upstairs with us, we didn't hold out much hope for him staying downstairs with her. However, he made no attempt to go up the stairs, so we gave them both a sleepy-time chewy and headed off to bed.

We lay awake, listening for Tia – or Louie, but it stayed quiet, and eventually, for the first time in a long time, we fell asleep *without* Louie tripping the light fandango on our bed. He was busy downstairs making the new member of our family feel at home – probably teaching her some bad habits too!

Beautiful Tia

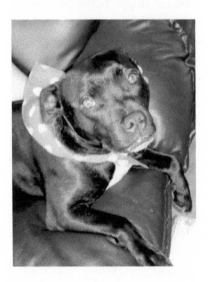

TIA FINDS HER PAWS

During the days that followed, Tia's character started to shine through little by little. She really was a sweet natured little soul. She paid more, and demanded more attention, but best of all, her little tail had found its wag! She started offering her paw for her dinner/chewies, but it was more of a high five than a paw shake and made us both smile. So, instead of asking her for a paw, we say, 'five Tia' and she'll willingly oblige.

We walked them together, and soon they were chasing each other around the fields. It was so lovely to see. Things were improving at home too; her appetite had returned, and she was settling down a treat. Louie had even plucked up courage to tease her, by taking her toy, and then standing in front of her till she chased him away! It's so funny when it happens. She curls up her top lip, and slowly, the rest of her mouth joins in. It looks like she's doing an 'Elvis' impersonation!

Her crate however, remained empty, she wouldn't even look at it. Maybe she associated it with sadness? Each night, her and Louie snuggled down on the settee (yes, I know they shouldn't really, but I'd rather they had the settee than our bed!)

Christmas was only a few weeks away, and soon the madness

would begin, however, there was something far more important happening before Christmas arrived. We were having a party!

Terry and Marcia had stayed on in Thailand for a couple of weeks to relax after the mayhem of the wedding, and they were going to stop off for a few days on their way back to Houston. Iain and me had organised a get together at our house, for all the family who were unable to go to Thailand. It would be interesting to see how Tia would react to all the strangers in her house, and believe me, they don't get much stranger than my family. In the nicest way of course!

Terry and Marcia arrived on a bitterly cold day – it must have felt like the Antarctic to them after the tropics! Louie was pleased to see them, it was a long time since he'd last seen them, but I'm sure he remembered them; he was bouncing off the walls!

When the rest of the family arrived, we asked them to give Tia some space, and wait for her to go to them. I needn't have worried, she soon appeared amongst us, and even gave permission for everyone to rub her tummy!

It was wonderful to have all our family together – busy – but wonderful. Sadly, it doesn't happen too often, but we make the most of it when we can. We had the most brilliant day, which seemed to whizz by, and all too soon, it was time to say goodbye to our visitors. Terry and Marcia stayed for a couple more days, then flew off to Texas, where their new, married life was waiting for them.

Christmas seemed a little bit of an anti-climax the week after in view of everything that had happened earlier in the year. The dogs amused us opening their presents, and although some of you may think it a complete waste of money, knowing how long squeakies last in Louie's mouth, believe me, it's worth every penny to watch him kill them.

As per usual, it wasn't long before the assassination was complete!

It was a quiet, peaceful day. No kids this year, except for the furry kind. Iain's parents joined us for a fairly relaxed lunch – compared to what it's usually like, but it was lovely for a change! After they left, we lazed on the settee with the dogs (they let us share it with them!) and watched Christmas telly through our eyelids!

CANINE CRAVINGS AND A SACK OF GRAVEL

A couple of weeks into the New year, we decided to dismantle Tia's crate. She'd shown no interest in it whatsoever, so it would have to go. Thinking we might find a use for it one day, we put it in the garage along with the rest of the stuff we don't need but can't throw away! Like a lot of other people, our garage doesn't house a car – it just collects 'stuff'.

Apart from the crate, there was something else she didn't like; having her photo taken. Every time I pointed a camera or my phone at her, she would run and hide. Iain said she maybe thought I was trying to steal her soul! Even if she was asleep, she seemed to know what I was doing, and the minute I pointed anything in her direction, her eyes would blink open, and she would run away.

The photos I did manage to capture were either blurry – she'd move at the crucial moment, or I'd catch her with her head hung down looking sad or waiting for something awful to occur! We'd have to work on that, she was such a beautiful girl, we wanted lots of photos of her. Louie, on the other hand, would lie on his back at the drop of a hat! Those long legs flailing in the air, exhibiting his bits for all and sundry!

January is the month we celebrate our wedding anniversary,

and something to look forward to after the come down from Christmas. This year, my sister Christine and St. Nicola were joining us for lunch to celebrate. Our local pub does a mean Sunday lunch, and Iain didn't need any persuading! We were leaving the dogs at home but seeing as how Louie was getting obsessed with Tia's rear end, we decided to split them up.

Lee had told us she wouldn't be in season until April, but Louie was getting more desperate by the day! Obviously, having a male and female dog, the question of Grand-puppies arose! Iain gave that idea a big thumbs down, which I agreed with, but for different reasons. His main one being that I wouldn't want to part with any puppies. Can't imagine why he would think that!

After taking advice and doing our homework, we decided that overall, it would be better to have Tia spayed and sooner rather than later in view of Louie's behaviour, so booked her in for the end of January.

When our anniversary day arrived, we put the dogs in separate rooms – Tia upstairs, Louie down, and set off to the pub with Christine and Nicky. We were only gone for a couple of hours, but we were in for a shock when we got back. The four of us were flabbergasted at what we saw.

Louie was nowhere to be seen, but we could hear him. Little devil had managed to get upstairs and was at the bedroom door where Tia was. His paws were covered with blood, because he'd almost scratched and bitten a hole through the door! Thankfully, Tia was still where we'd left her, but the door was a proper mess, and Louie was exhausted!

It reminded me of a time many years ago, when our gorgeous Labrador, the original Spike (aka Mr. Wigs) went on a recce trying to find himself a little loving. He'd sneaked out of the garden undetected and ended up being locked in a shed at a rather posh house in the village. I was mortified when the lady of the house called to tell me my Labrador was 'frolicking' with her bitches! Thankfully, Louie was still in the house, but the bedroom door would need some serious attention!

As we tried to bathe Louie's paws, I told him that his pocket money would be suspended indefinitely, to cover the cost of repairing the door! We couldn't really shout at him (but boy I so wanted to!) after all, he was just following his urges. Yes, well those urges might just have to be chopped off if he didn't improve after Tia's spaying!

We arranged to have the appointment brought forward, and took her in for the op. The Vet told us that Tia was much nearer to her season than we'd thought, so it was a good job we'd taken her then and not waited till nearer April. She went on to say it was possible all the upheaval could have brought it on. Thankfully, after a few days of spoilings and cuddles, she was well on the mend.

BBFs

The coming of Spring seemed to spur us both into doing some jobs on the house. One of these was the driveway. Over the past few years, the gravel had slowly depleted, goodness knows where it's gone, but, aided and abetted by two Staffies playing with balls, it was looking decidedly sparse in several places. Iain ordered two, huge bags of gravel and invited Chris for the weekend!

Unfortunately, I can't help too much with heavy jobs any more, but I *can* make copious cups of tea – and supervise. Iain just loves it when I supervise!

Chris arrived before the gravel, and entertained us by tormenting Grendel, who, as always, was delighted to see him. They're as daft as each other and had us in stitches clowning around.

The gravel arrived bright and early the following morning. Louie was up at the window in the conservatory gobbing off at the driver. He was bursting to get out, but we made sure the door was locked. The last thing we needed was him interfering. Tia, who was laying on the settee, seemed only concerned about the amount of sleep she was missing out on because of the disturbance! She was quite happy to let Louie be on duty.

Once it was in the garden, and the driver had left, we let Louie go out and he made a beeline for one of the sacks and jumped right on top of it. For whatever reason, he decided it was his, and set about stamping the paw of authority on it by digging it, then peeing all over it! Obviously, there was no way of stopping him in mid-flow, so we just had to wait.

So, there we stood, shovels poised, ready to fling the gravel over the driveway, but Louie refused to move. He really is a proper bonehead sometimes! We got him to move to the other sack, and he cocked his leg again, only this time, I think it was phantom peeing as there was no wet gravel. After removing a few shovels full, they attempted to upend the sack, but it was still too heavy.

When Louie saw what they were doing, he decided he was going to join in. He got one of the corners in his mouth and set about destroying it – and it worked! He pulled so hard, the side began to give, and the gravel started to trickle out from the sack. When Iain and Chris were ready for the next one, Chris just told

Louie to 'have it!' and once again, he ripped the side of the sack. Tia watched from the window; she had no intention of getting involved in anything that required her to move! She no longer let Louie take advantage of her, she has her own way of sorting him out. She waits until he's asleep, then snipes up, grabs one of his back legs, and tries to drag him along with it! She doesn't leave go, even when he stands up. He looks a right plonker just standing there while Tia tries to bite his leg off! He's such a wuss – the epitome of pathetic!

With a little help from the Louster, they had the driveway done in no time at all. Pity I couldn't get him to do the housework too! His penchant to rip things has no limits, and whenever we have a delivery, we have to be sure that he's out of the way, because he'll have it the minute you turn your back!

Louie with his gravel!

There's another incident that still makes me laugh…

One of our neighbours had had some lino fitted and thought the dogs might like the cardboard tube to play with. They just loved playing with anything they could rip up, and thinking it might occupy them for a while, I said yes. What I hadn't considered was the size - the empty tube - must have been well over six feet long!

This should be interesting!

They set about it straight away! This was really comical to watch, because neither of them could take it from the other one, and the ends were too big to fit in their mouths. After a while, with an end apiece, they started dancing round the driveway. That in itself was hysterical to watch, but funnier still was the fact that their whining/growling noises were echoing through the tube and they couldn't understand what it was! At first, they seemed to think it was something inside the tube that was making the noise, but they just couldn't figure out how to get inside it.

They kept it up for hours before realising the tube was empty. It was eventually ripped up into bite-size pieces, and kept them happy for a couple of days, but like everything else they have, Lou's-tube ended up in the bin!

LouTube!

VISITING SAM

Since I started writing Fully Staffed, a lot of things have happened; some not too good, some very good, and some amazing! Iain has now fully retired (not sure which category that goes in!) and we are both enjoying our retirement.

We watched our beloved Grandson, Sam marry a beautiful young lady – Michaela, and have been blessed with three great grandchildren. Ruby, Emily and baby Zachary. I understand Grandchildren are the reward for not killing your own kids! We love them all to bits!

Sam is in the military, so we don't get to see them as often as we'd like, so we make the most of it when we can get together.

We visited them quite recently and decided to take the dogs with us if we could find a dog friendly hotel close to where they live. Neither of us like the idea of kennels, and we didn't want to descend on the kids with the dogs. Luckily, we found Worplesdon Place, just a ten- minute drive away from where they live.

Set well back from the main road in lovely grounds, it was a perfect location. There's a special area of the hotel designated for guests with dogs, or in our case, guests with pests! Our room had patio doors at the back, which opened into part of the surrounding grounds, and providing there are no other dogs around, you can just let them out to do their doggy stuff. You can even take them into the pub area while you eat, providing they are well behaved (that's us out then!)

The first morning when we gave them their breakfast outside our patio doors, placing their bowls on a little wall just outside our door, that separated the footpath from the garden. It was just the right height, as they eat from a raised dog bowls.

After they'd eaten, Iain took them for a trot around the gardens while I was getting ready. While he was out, I discovered we had neighbours, as from the corner of my eye, I saw something by the window. I almost jumped out of my skin to see it was another dog, and said dog walked right into our room! It was a beautiful Japanese Samoyed, looking as though it had been freshly spray- painted – a little white cloud, it was immaculate. Thankfully, her mum came looking for her, and after a quick hello and bit of fussing she took her away. Just as well, because I could hear my two causing havoc and mayhem somewhere outside, which meant they could be on their way back, and they wouldn't be too thrilled to see another dog at their house!

The following day gave us another surprise. We'd given the dogs their breakfast – al fresco again, only we forgot to bring in their bowls. Hearing Tia bump into the window made us jump, and a barking frenzy began as Louie joined her. The Samoyed from next door was out; not only was she out, she was licking out their bowls! We tried to close the curtains, but they were having none of it, and the scrummage by the window went on. Concerned that they might pull the whole lot down, we quickly opened the curtains again.

The Samoyed took no notice of the two crazy canines jumping up and sliding down the door, which was now covered in dog yuk! She seemed to know they were all bark and no bite, so took her time licking the bowls. I'm amazed she found anything to lick after Miss Piggy (Tia) had finished with it! Any of the guests that didn't already know there were two Staffys staying at the hotel certainly would do now!

Next morning, we thought we'd take the dogs with us to breakfast to see how they'd behave…

The area where dogs are allowed was almost empty, so we found a seat near a window close to the door, ordered our food and sat back to enjoy our cup of tea. The dogs settled down under the table, but soon, the peace was shattered. The dogs jumped up, almost upended the table, and frightened the life out of us. There was tea everywhere!

While trying to hide our embarrassment and mop up the tea, we looked around, trying to fathom out what it was that had set them off barking, but there was nothing to see not hear. We settled them down, called them a few names, and waited for our breakfasts to arrive. However, within minutes, the silence was broken yet again with a repeat performance!

"Perhaps I'd better take them back to the room before any of the other diners at the opposite end choke on their breakfast or have a heart attack!"

"Might be a good idea" I agreed "but make sure you close the curtains!"

Just as Iain was about to leave, the cause of the barking came to light. Each time the kitchen had a meal ready to collect, they pressed a bell to alert a member of staff to collect it. This bell sounded exactly like our doorbell, and they just couldn't contain themselves - they wanted to see who was coming in. Thank goodness there wasn't anyone coming in at the time, it would have put them right off their Full English!

On our final morning, we closed the curtains, left them in the room and had a tranquil, leisurely breakfast!

We looked after the children that day, as Sam was on a parade, and Michaela was going to watch. We were both out of practice – three children and two dogs wore us out. The dogs loved playing with Ruby and Emily but drew the line when it came to having lipstick put on, so Grandad got the makeover! Baby Zachary slept through most of it.

Later that day, it was time for us to say goodbye. The kids were travelling to Wales that night, as Sam was on parade the next day. I'm so glad our service days are over!

FINAL WORD?

It's now almost Spring 2019, we've come a long way since those early days with Spike and Jake, and still miss their antics – I guess we always will. Having felt somewhat guilty initially for having another dog after Jake, I have to say that now I try not to dwell on it too much. Louie helped no end to ease the pain of losing Spike, in fact, he's like him in so many ways. Being round the bend at the top of the list! I think Spike and Jake would be proud of us for taking on two doggies, who for very different reasons, had to find another home.

Louie and Tia are still BBFs, and he must love her, as she has her own key to his office. They can usually be found up there guarding the garden/house/road/village/ - it all belongs to them!

Tails from the office

So, here we are, the end of another book – almost…

My very first attempt at putting pen to paper (or fingers to keys!) was a story about Jakes' first year told from how I (*imagined*) would be his point of view; how he felt about leaving his litter and getting a new mum and dad. At the time, I had neither the confidence, nor time to complete it.

However, now I have a little more time to play with, I managed to finish it and thought you might like to read it.

So, without further ado, I give you…

JAKE'S JOURNAL

*Most fairy stories begin with 'Once upon a time' – but not this one! There will be no fairies or clichés in my story; (I have no intentions of leaving my comfort zone, riding any fairground attractions, and I won't be participating in any journeys!) However, there **will** be dogs, and I believe we are far more interesting than fairies...*

Allow me to introduce myself:

My name is Jake, and I am a Staffordshire Bull Terrier. I believe I am a 'Red' colour, but that means absolutely nothing to me. I do know however, that I am a rather handsome chap, even though I say so myself, and I have often heard it said by other people too, so I must be simply gorgeous!

I live in a small village in something they call Rutland. The family I live with were looking for a pack-leader, and I was more than capable of fulfilling the role. This is how I found my pack...

In the beginning, there were six of us – two girls and four boys. We arrived in the early hours of an April morning, which just happened to be Meg's (our canine mum's) birthday. What better gift could she have had, than six hungry, beautiful little pups!

Poor Meg, she had probably been planning a quiet day of pampering and relaxation, with a few treats on the side, followed by a succulent, little feast for dinner. We soon put paid to that!

I don't remember much about that day you understand, it's just that I heard the people talking about us. However, I **do** remember later on, I would awaken to find one of my siblings' legs or snouts stuck in my ear, and the others sleeping in the strangest positions where they'd just flopped down. Terribly undignified, but we were only tiny fur babies then, not much bigger than hamsters so I hear. You know, looking back, those first few weeks fairly took it out of me, but somehow, I managed to find enough time to eat and sleep in between all the naps, siestas and snoozes.

Each day that passed, saw us growing in size and confidence. One day, Meg told us that we had much to learn, and not much time to do it. Obviously, being the brains of the outfit, I had already learned a few, basic tips so was one paw ahead!

First up – best fed comes to mind and getting in first means you get prime dining position. I liked to be near Meg's head, that way, there weren't too many legs and tails to contend with.

Lying on top of the others was a good trick too, as it meant when Meg arrived to feed us, their movement was my alarm bell, so I was first in the queue for the chow. Quite ingenious don't you think. I also learned that if I make a lot of noise, one of the people will come and give me a cuddle.

Providing the others aren't looking, (I **do** have my street cred to consider!) I snuggle right up to them. I quite like this snuggling thing with the people, but they don't half smell funny. Meg said it was nothing to worry about, most of the people smell and we'd soon get used to it given time. Maybe so, but it will never beat the whiff of the whelping box!

Meg was a good tutor, firm but fair, she wasn't averse to a quick nip on the ear if things got too rowdy. What she was about to teach us was proper, serious stuff, so we'd best give her our undivided attention for a while. This was easier said than done considering at that time, collectively, we had a retention span of a goldfish!

She began by explaining, that this was **her** home and **her** pack, but for some strange reason, the people she lives with consider themselves to be 'pack leaders'! (I know, incredible isn't it?) However, the benefits of letting them believe they **are** the leaders will be many if we just comply with this outlandish idea. We would need to learn some skilful tactics in order to convince them we thought of them as leaders!

We would only be staying with Meg long enough for her to teach us the basic guidelines of Canine Etiquette… Somewhere out there, there was a pack just waiting for the arrival of a new leader, it was just a question of finding the right one. Meg said this made perfect sense, how can we all be pack leaders if we stay with the same pack?

Not only would she teach us basic survival skills, she would teach us the manipulative techniques we would need in the human world. Then, we would have no trouble finding a loving home, because after following her instructions, we would all be canine connoisseurs of persuasion!

One day, Meg gathered us all together to tell us we were ready to learn some new life skills, or instincts. Instincts are a very important part of a canines' life, and we would need to learn when to act on them and what to do when we felt them. This would begin tomorrow when we were going to be weaned (I didn't like the sound of that) but, all it meant really, was that we would be eating the same sort of food that she did. I was gutted – I loved my milky!

True to her word, our 'weaning' process began the day after. Snouts in the air, we sniffed as the smell got closer, and we saw Meg's mum come with it. She had little bowls in her hands, which she laid on the floor of our box. We were all a little dubious of these bowl things, even though Meg had told us this was what weaning meant.

Meg's mum was waving us to go closer, then she put one of her paws in the bowl, covered it with the stuff inside and offered it to one of my brothers. He had a little lick, seemed to like it, so we all went for a lick. It wasn't what we were used to, but it was ok – ish. I still preferred my milk - guess I would just have to get used to it. I do hope Meg's mum isn't going to stick her paws in my food every day!

When we snuggled down to sleep that night, Meg told us there was another treat in store for us the next day, we were going to be going 'outside' Meg went outside a lot, we always knew when she'd been out because she had different smells on her. Nice different mind you, I wasn't the only one itching to get out for a serious sniff, we were all desperate to test drive our paws!

The next day, things didn't quite go according to plan. We had to reschedule our trip because of rain. Meg told us that rain was like the water we drink, but when it falls from the sky, they call it rain. Not a doggy's best friend, as it makes your coat wet, cold and smelly. Now, although smelly is good, the best place for any Staffy on a wet day, is curled up by a nice, warm fire stinking the house out! Sounds good to me, or it would do if I knew what a fire was?

The rain had gone away by the next day, so our excursion to the garden would take place after we'd had our breakfast with Meg. Oh boy, when the time came, we were all jostling to get out, and eager to see what was on the other side of the door. One of my little sister's didn't seem too thrilled to be going out, so I waited with her till she was ready to go, Aren't I just a little sweetie pie!

Our maiden voyage was very exciting, everything's SO big, a bit scary really. We stayed in our little group for a while, and then we followed our snouts and went our different ways. Meg was hovering around us, teaching us about the things in the garden – I was mesmerised! The floor smelled, looked and felt different! Meg told us this was grass, it was green, and we could also eat it if we had a poorly tummy. Anything that involves eating is good. This is also the place where we come when we need a wee or a poo. Seems the lady doesn't like it if you do your doggy business in the house. I can't think why?

The test drive was fine, my cornering needed a little fine tuning, but otherwise, I had a faultless round!

In between our sleeping, snoozing, napping and eating, Meg continued to give us the benefit of her wisdom, there was still so much to learn. She expanded on the 'family' lesson and told us there were many different forms of families, and no matter which one we ended up with, as long as we were loved and cared for, that was all that mattered. What about 'adored and pampered?'

One day, just as we'd all settled down for our Siesta, Meg alerted us that we had people coming to see us. I hope they weren't going to disturb one of my many afternoon naps!

These weren't just any people; they were potential Mum & Dad people who just might be looking for a leader. As usual, I was first in the queue, and my pack mates looked on in envy, as I pushed my way to the front and flashed my credentials their way! I knew what was expected of me, so I tried to convince them they need look no further – I was the one they wanted. I had all the desirable qualities they were looking for-: Faithful – fearless – noble, with oodles of cuteness thrown in! Although I got some strokes and snuggles from them, they seemed far more interested in one of my sisters. I know. How could they even consider fussing someone else when I was there? I decided then that I didn't want to be the leader of their pack!

As we grew a little bigger, we continued to enjoy life in our little box. The weaning was going down a storm, but we still missed our milky! We looked forward to our trips to the garden and enjoyed our rough and tumble sessions, though they were getting a little more energetic now. More people came to see us, and we soon got used to being picked up and examined!

Eventually, the day arrived when someone came just for ME! We *were having a little play-time in the corner of our box, when I heard a voice say, "which one of you is called Jake?"*

As usual, I was first in the queue as the people crouched down to stroke us. Meg's mum was with them, and before I knew it, I was lifted up and put in the lady's arms. She said

"Hello Jake, what a handsome boy you are. Would it be okay with you if we took you to live with us, and be your new mum and dad? We'll have SO much fun! We'll go for long walks in the woods, take you to the seaside, take very good care of you and we'll love you to bits!"

Where do I sign?

There was a man with her, and he wanted to hold me too! I was quite enjoying all this fuss – yes, I think I could get used to this. Eventually, I was put back in the box with my siblings and the people left. Didn't they want me?

Meg explained to me that I wasn't quite old enough to leave yet, but she was pretty sure I was going to be the leader of their pack! I liked the sound of that – even if they did smell funny.

They came again the following week for more snuggles. They brought me a present too, my very own blanket – I'm a lucky pup for sure!

HOMEWARD BOUND

At long last, the day finally arrived for me to leave my pack. A couple of them had already gone, and, although it was a bit sad, it was more exciting as we were all going to be Pack Leaders!

The people that I was going to take charge of didn't come until after we'd had our morning nap, but I was all ready to go the minute they arrived. Meg's mum lifted me out of the box, put my blanket around me, and put me in the arms of my new 'mum' – I'm sure I'll get used to her funny smell! Meg and the siblings who were left all came to the front of the box, tails wagging to say goodbye. I was finally on my way!

We got to the car, and I sat on my mum's knee in the back. This was a whole, new experience for me. I'd seen and heard these car things go past Meg's house, but I'd never been in one. To be honest, I didn't really like it too much. I felt a bit yukky, but my new mum kept snuggling me, and that made it okay.

After what seemed a long time, we stopped, dad got out, opened this big gate, got back in the car, then we started going backwards! Oh I didn't like that one little bit, but It didn't last long, and soon, me and my new mum were out of the car – my new home at last!

She put me down on the floor and let me have a look around. She was telling me all sorts of things, but I didn't have a clue what she was going on about, I had more important things to attend to, one of which *couldn't wait a minute longer! I squatted down and relieved myself – I would find a special spot later, but this would do for now.*

Seems it was right in front of the back door – and their problem is?

My new garden

We walked around the garden together, me in front, of course – no time like the present to show them who's the leader! It was much bigger than my last one, and there were lots of smells begging to be sniffed. My mum showed me a ball, and kept saying 'Jake's ball' but, she didn't give it to me. Instead, she threw it to dad, and he threw it back to her. I think they expected me to do something, but I didn't know what? Anyway, they seemed to be enjoying themselves with my ball, so I left them to it, and continued my trip around the garden.

Next, mum lifted me up, and took me inside my new home. First of all, she took me (to what I now know to be the kitchen) and showed me my very own bed, complete with my special blanket. She put me into the bed and said 'Jake's bed' I was ready for a nap after all the excitement, I'd missed out on my forty winks that day, so I snuggled down for a swift snooze.

When I woke up, my mum had some food ready for me – and it was **all** for me! It was nice not having to fend off my rivals for the dish. Afterwards, I was allowed to sit between them on their settee and passed the rest of my busy day catching up on some much-needed sleep!

The following day, some strange noise coming from the corner woke me (it was the boiler, but I didn't know that then) and after listening for a while, I went off to find out what was causing it. There was no mum or dad around, I wondered where they were – they wouldn't have left me surely? I ventured into the hall and found the staircase. Boy, there was an awful lot of stairs for a little pup! I'd seen stairs in the garden at Meg's house, but not this many. Well, nothing ventured…

I managed to get up most of them, but there was a really big one near the top, and it was just too much for my little legs. I hate to say, but I started howling – only a low-level howl, but I needed mum or dad to help me. Sure enough, within seconds, dad was there, and I was being lifted up in the air. He took me into this room where mum was in their bed. Wow, I couldn't believe the size of it -it was much bigger than mine! Surely there's room for me in there?

'Look who I found at the top of the stairs' he said to mum as he passed me to her.

'Hello, my little guy, what are you doing climbing up all those stairs? You could have fallen and hurt yourself'

Ah, but I didn't.

I lay between them and let them rub my tummy, it was quite nice actually. Oh yes, this is the life for me! All I need now was some chow! Downstairs, dad took me to the back garden, and I dashed off to find a good place for my morning ablutions. There were plenty of places to choose from, and I soon found just the spot, where I settled down to attend to business! When I went back in the house, my food was waiting for me in the little bowl – this is the life.

As the days passed, I whipped mum and dad into a nice routine. They were coming on a treat and were very easy to train actually. I always knew where they were – right around the tip of my tail!

Just after I'd woken up one morning, mum said we were going to go for a little ride in the car to get my injections at the vets. I didn't like the sound of that, and I didn't like the car, but played along with her. Injection was a new word for me, as was vet. I wonder what they mean. We didn't stay in the car very long and were soon at the vets. The smells in there were amazing, not all of them pleasing to a little pup, but boy, there was some serious sniffing to be had! Thing was, mum didn't put me down, oh I was desperate to get stuck in, but no amount of wriggling and squirming persuaded her to put me on the floor. Mmmm!

A man came out of a room and said 'Jake please'

'Good morning' mum said to him 'beautiful day out there isn't it?' she said.

Once in his little room, he proceeded to check me out, while mum chatted away telling him what a good boy I was, and how easy I'd been to toilet train.

Oh please!!

Before I knew what was happening, he grabbed the fur on the back of my head and put something on my neck. I didn't really feel anything, and after the vet telling me I was a 'good boy' we were on our way back home. Shame I didn't get five minutes for a good sniff of that floor! Maybe next time...

When dad came home that day, there was a whiff of excitement in the air because we were all going for a walk!! Yeah, our very first outing. I was beginning to think they didn't want me to take them out! Meg had told us about walks or walkies., and about the lead they would put on me so I wouldn't lose them. I was beside myself as they opened the huge gate and I led them out.

First impression – big! Everything was so big, but I wasn't worried, I was leader of the pack – fierce, faithful and unafraid! I let them take the reins that first day, just so I could get my bearings. Off up the street we went, there were so many things to see, most of which were completely new to me, but I would soon get used to them. We had a busy road to cross at the top, and I must confess, I was a bit anxious. The cars were moving pretty fast, and they looked so big to a young pup! I sensed they were dangerous, so I thought I ought to get mum to stop till they'd all gone. As I stopped, she asked me to sit, she must be scared of the cars too, but after a few minutes, we safely crossed over, and headed to the fields. Yes, I shall look forward to my daily walkies.

As we walked along a little grassy path, the aroma of a new smell wafted to my nose. I tried to sniff out what it was, and very soon I saw the reason for the smell.

It was the biggest dog in the world! Absolutely massive, and it was heading my way - I don't mind confessing, the 'brave' bit deserted me for a while. I needn't have worried though, as mum told me this colossal dog was actually a horse. As it came to the fence, mum stroked its humongous snout. It seemed to like this, and seeing as how mum wasn't afraid of it, I thought I'd best let her see that I wasn't.

THE HORSE DOG!

Soon after my first venture into the big outdoors, I heard mum and dad talking about puppy classes. Were they getting another puppy? I hope not, because I'm the pack leader here, and I certainly didn't need puppy classes.

Wrong! They had decided that I needed to learn to be 'sociable' and

we would be going once a week. I wasn't best pleased – puppy classes –
I ask you!

They took me for my first lesson in 'sociable' a few days later when
dad came home. It meant we had to go in the car, so I wasn't very
happy to begin with, but once we arrived, there was a lovely surprise
waiting for me. There, also learning to be sociable were the rest of my
siblings! Yeah, we were all together again, except for Meg, who was far
too polished to need classes, and one of my sisters who had left the area.
It was sniff bliss as we greeted each other.

We all sat together in a corner of the room, and my mum said we
ought to be called The Staffia! I have no idea what that meant, but all
the people with my siblings thought it was funny. At first, we just had
to walk around the room – easy peasy, **and** I was given a chewy at the
end. Next, we had to do the same, but without mum on her lead. I could
sense that she was a bit nervous, but she did ok, and I got a chewy! As
you've probably guessed, it didn't take me long to figure out that every
time I did what she said, I was given a chewy. These classes aren't so
bad after all!

Then, just as I was getting used to it, we didn't go any more. I did
get a certificate though, and mum read it and said 'this is to certify that
Jake and Linda have completed a course of puppy training, and Jake is
the smartest puppy ever'

(Okay, so it didn't really say the last bit, but mum and dad think I
am, and that'll do for me!)

As the days passed, and I continued to grow in size, knowledge and
confidence, but there was still much for me to learn. Some of the many
things out in the big wide world, are not doggy friendly.

One night as I went for my sleepy time patrol of the garden, I came
across a new smell. When I went over to investigate, I noticed a
strange, new smell coming from near the shed. I followed the smell
around the shed and came across this little odd -looking ball. Well, I
gave it a good sniffing, but it didn't move. I gave it a nudge with my
paw, and still, it didn't move. Finally, I shoved my snout right at it –
and got the biggest shock of my life, as the darn thing stuck to my

mouth! Ouch! It didn't half sting, and no amount of pawing could get rid of it. I howled until mum and dad came running out.

Dad lifted me up, and I heard mum say, 'oh my God, it's a hedgehog, there's a hedgehog stuck in his mouth!' I wasn't really interested in its name, I just wanted them to get it out because it was hurting me. I was squirming around trying to get rid of it, but it was stuck! Dad managed to free it, but it left some of its stingy things in my mouth, which didn't half smart when they were pulled out.

Back indoors, mum bathed my poorly mouth (I must have lost at least a pint of blood!) after which gave me lots of snuggles and a little chewy. Chewies make everything better! As for that hedgehog – he won't get away so easily next time! I'll be ready for him.

When it was nice and warm outside, I enjoyed lying in the sunshine, toasting my tummy. Mum put a little mat out for me, which was far more comfortable for me. If I got too warm, I sauntered into the kitchen to lie on the nice, cold floor. She also put this plastic thing out in my garden and filled it with water – you won't believe this, but she expected me to get in it!

Not...

A...

Chance!

I was determined not to look, but she kept shouting me. I tried ignoring her, but she was having none of it. If I was going to stand any chance of my afternoon siesta, I had to shut her up, so I strolled across and took a look. When I got there, she said 'Jakey's pool'

Really – I think not!

As I sloped off, she splashed some water at me, but I was unimpressed. She splashed me some more, but I remained unimpressed – and now wet!

After a few minutes of stand-off, I ambled back to my cosy rug. Jakey's pool or not, there was no way I was going near that thing again – not while she was next to it anyway.

You know, these humans have some very strange sayings, none of which seem to be true. It can get very confusing sometimes! One day, I was in my bed having my elevenses, when I heard mum say, 'it's raining cats and dogs!' Oh wow! This I just **had** to see!

I knew what raining was but raining with cats and dogs – that was a whole new experience! I was out of my bed in a flash, and after a little skid at the corner of the living room floor, I arrived at the back door. I looked out, but there was no sign of any cats or dogs. Maybe I wasn't quick enough, and I'd missed them? I sat and waited, but all I saw was rain – lots and lots of it. After a while I gave up and went back to my nice warm bed. Perhaps it was too wet for the cats and dogs after all... Later on, mum came into the kitchen, and said to dad that the weather was so wet, it wasn't fit to turn a dog out.

You can see why I get confused...

Then there was Christmas. I kept hearing the word over and over again. Mum told me if I'd been a good boy, then 'Santa Paws' would be bringing me some toys, but more important – chewies! I liked the sound of that. As for being good, well, I was feeling very pleased with myself: mum and dad's training was coming on in leaps and bounds, and I kept on doing as mum and dad asked me to do, so yes, I figure I'm not just a good boy, I'm quite amazing!

As it grew closer to Santa Paws time, mum started doing strange things in the house. She came downstairs with some huge boxes that had loads of curious looking things inside. She would need my help to empty them of course, and this gave me chance to investigate. I watched in amazement, intrigued at all the stuff coming out of them. She put a long sparkly thing around my neck, told me it was tinsel, and I looked gorgeous. I know that already! I didn't need any tinsel to confirm it, so set about getting rid of it. In doing so, I managed to get bits of it everywhere!

I was fascinated to see them bring a tree inside – how very thoughtful of them! They didn't need to dress it up for me, but then, I guess they thought I was worth it! I wasn't sure I'd be able to cock my leg that high though...

The next day, she appeared with another box, and put it on the floor. Smaller than the rest, I had to go and check it out. I gave it a good sniff, and found nothing interesting, but when I biffed it, I almost jumped out of my fur! The top shot open, and this head appeared covered in white fluffy stuff wearing a red hat. When it started singing, I heard that Christmas word again, 'we wish you a merry Christmas…'

I was going to have to have it! Santa Paws would be hearing about this!

I lunged forward and grabbed it with my mouth. 'We wish you a merry Christmas' was going to get what for! As I ran to my bed with it, mum chased after me, telling me to 'leave it'. No way, it's my job to protect her, and I wasn't letting this thing scare her like it had me! Once she realised I wasn't going to give up easily, she brought out one of my favourite chewies – I dropped the hairy, white head thing immediately! I'm just a sucker for a nice, little chew – chewies over-ride everything! Mum put the head in the box on top of a cupboard out of my reach. Ah well, some you lose.

Just before Christmas arrived, people started coming to my house. I hadn't met any of them before, so I would have to give them a good sniffing before bestowing the paw of approval. They all made a fuss of me, and of course, I let them! One of these people brought another dog called Spike, who was much bigger than me, and didn't smell like he was from round here. Mum and dad seemed to know him and made a big fuss – I wasn't sure I approved of this! He came over and gave me a good sniffing, then poked me a few times with his huge snout. I wasn't going to stand for that – I had to make sure he knew this was **my** house, and not his, so I biffed him back, but it didn't go down too well, and he nipped my ear!

Ouch, that hurt! I howled and mum came and picked me up. There was a little blood, but nothing serious. Mum kept me on her lap for a while after, so I was safe – it also meant that I could stick my tongue out at Spike whenever he came near! I would be making sure he was on the naughty list when Santa Paws came.

When the Christmas arrived, I was happy to see there were lots of things wrapped up in paper just for me. Oh, I just love tearing paper up! I wasn't interested in what was inside, I just liked the paper. Me and Spike had lots of fun ripping up the paper, maybe we'll be friends after all…

There was lots of fun, lots of laughter and lots food at Christmas. Me and Spike had a special dinner that day, and afterwards as I lay dozing, Spike came and laid beside me. He told me he was going to teach me a few things I might find useful before he left, one of which was scrounging! Sometimes, (as we'd just found out) people food is much tastier than ours, but for some reason, they don't like sharing it with us, except on special occasions like today. Shame really, I would share my food with mum and dad anytime, but they never ask.

Wanna bite?

This is where scrounging comes in, and he told me to watch and learn. He took up his favoured position, (scrounge mode) and set about demonstrating the art of scrounging. After a while, his dad called him over, shook his paw, and gave him a little bite of what he was eating. I was in awe! I couldn't wait to try!

I walked over to my mum and tried to emulate Spikes actions. She ignored me, so I went a little closer, but no joy. Eventually, she said "no Jake, it's not for puppys" I was gutted.

After watching my feeble attempts, Spike said I needed to work on my technique, and not give up so easily. Sometimes, they'd give you a little morsel just to get rid of you!

Food for thought maybe...

A few days later, Spike and his dad went back to their house, and left us in peace. Mum was being busy, so I went to lay by the back door and watched the world go by. I must have nodded off, because when I woke up, there was loads of stuff all around the garden! It wasn't rain – I know what rain is (and I don't like it!) When mum saw it, she said 'look Jake, it's snowing!' Ah, so this is snow then – this would need further investigation!

One paw was all I needed! It was very cold and wet – no way was I going outside in that - not voluntarily anyway. No, the best place for me when the snow comes, is in front of the nice, cosy fire now -I know what a fire is!

Sometime later, the urge to attend to doggy business came over me, and I just had to go outside. The snow was quite deep now – it was so cold on my tummy, so I nipped round to where their car is, did my thing (very quickly!) and dashed back to the warmth of the fire. Ahhhh...

I'm getting quite a big boy now, and in a few months it will be my birthday, so mum says – I hope it involves chewies! All in all, life here is pretty good. I walk mum and dad every day, get fed regularly, and have lots of cuddles, chewies and treats.

I've learned quite a lot of things during my first year and would like to share my interpretation of them with you.

"raining cats and dogs" means even though there's loads of rain about, there won't be any cats and dogs falling from the sky!

"Hair of the dog" isn't always a bad thing and can sometimes make you feel better.

"You can't teach an old dog new tricks" I'm sure my mate Spike will sort that out.

"The tail wagging the dog" yeah right – it's never going to happen!

'Every dog has it's day" shouldn't that be every day needs a dog?

"In the dog-house" – (where dad sometimes hangs out) is somewhere I really don't want to be, but could end up there if I go

"Barking up the wrong tree"

"Let sleeping dogs' lie" means *don't disturb me if I'm having my nap.*

As for "dog's dinner" well, for me, it's a sight to behold.

But, by far the most important thing I've learned, is that through all the years that have gone before, and all of the ones still to come, we are, and always will be...

Mans' best friend.

I couldn't agree more...

Love, Jake x x x

ACKNOWLEDGMENTS

I must begin by saying an enormous thank you to my husband, and partner in crime – Iain. For standing beside me through good days and bad, ups, downs, and tearing out hair days! I love you

My sons Terry and Chris, for providing me with such funny, unintentional material. You are my world. Moon & back...

A massive thank you to my little sister, Beverley, who hopefully, won't choke me when she sees I included her 'hissy fit'! Christine, Nicky and everyone else – you're all mad, but I wouldn't have it any other way.

A huge thanks to Gordon, my wonderful father-in-law, for all his help and support – from the first read through, to the friendly critic and everything in between!

Once again, my sincere thanks to a brilliant author and dear friend, Brian L Porter. Thanks for being so generous with your time, advice and patience. I am truly grateful for all your help, expertise and guidance down this sometimes, rocky path!

To all at Oakham Veterinary Hospital, thanks for everything.

Many thanks to Debra Poole - editor extraordinaire! We had some fun and games with this one, but got there in the end. I appreciate your kind comments and patience!

Grateful thanks to The Pet Blood Bank U.K. in Loughborough, for the amazing service you provide. Special thanks to Maureen Reid, whose help was immensely beneficial. Also, Robert Pitchfork who got the ball rolling. A massive thanks also to Nicky, Boo's mum for giving me the lovely photos of her gorgeous boys. www.petbloodbankuk.org

A very special thank you to Mikka and the team at Creativia, for being so helpful and sprinkling their magic once again.

Finally, to the person reading this right now – thank you so much for buying my book!

ABOUT THE AUTHOR

Born in the North West of England, Linda Meredith grew up in Stalybridge until at the age of nineteen, she married a Royal Air Force serviceman, and moved to Yorkshire.

Having lived in several different places both here and abroad, she now lives in a tiny village in the beautiful Rutland countryside, with her husband Iain, two dogs and one rabbit. Their sons Terry and Chris have long since flown the nest, so their current kids have four legs, tails and whiskers.

She began writing many years ago, silly poems and stories for her sons. However, after being inspired by Brian L. Porter's book - Sasha, (a tale about the courage of his beautiful little Staffy) a couple of years ago, she decided, with lots of encouragement from her family and Brian, to write a book. The result of which is Fully Staffed.

Now retired, she is able to spend more time writing and doggy walking, and enjoying every minute!

Liberating Louie
ISBN: 978-4-86752-139-7

Published by
Next Chapter
1-60-20 Minami-Otsuka
170-0005 Toshima-Ku, Tokyo
+818035793528

21st July 2021

Lightning Source UK Ltd.
Milton Keynes UK
UKHW010627030821
388241UK00001B/203